AMERICA the BEAUTIFUL

MISSISSIPPI

By Robert Carson

Consultants

William A. Sullivan, Ph.D., Delta State University, Cleveland

Michael F. Beard, Historian, Mississippi Department of Archives and History, Jackson

David Sansing, Jr., McLaurin Middle School, Natchez Public Schools

Robert L. Hillerich, Ph.D., Bowling Green State University, Bowling Green, Ohio

 CHILDRENS PRESS ®

CHICAGO

Sunset over the Mississippi River

Project Editor: Joan Downing
Assistant Editor: Shari Joffe
Design Director: Margrit Fiddle
Typesetting: Graphic Connections, Inc.
Engraving: Liberty Photoengraving

Childrens Press®, Chicago
Copyright © 1989 by Regensteiner Publishing Enterprises, Inc.
All rights reserved. Published simultaneously in Canada.
Printed in the United States of America.
    7 8 9 10 R 98 97 96

Library of Congress Cataloging-in-Publication Data

Carson, Robert, 1932-
    America the beautiful. Mississippi / by Robert Carson.
        p.   cm.
    Includes index.
    Summary: Introduces the geography, history,
government, economy, industry, culture, historic sites,
and famous people of the Magnolia State.
    ISBN 0-516-00470-0
    1. Mississippi—Juvenile
literature. [1. Mississippi.] I.   Title.
F341.3.C35   1988   88-11747
976.2—dc19   CIP
                                                    AC

Cedar Grove, an antebellum mansion in Vicksburg, is surrounded by acres of formal gardens that contain fountains, courtyards, and gazebos such as this one.

TABLE OF CONTENTS

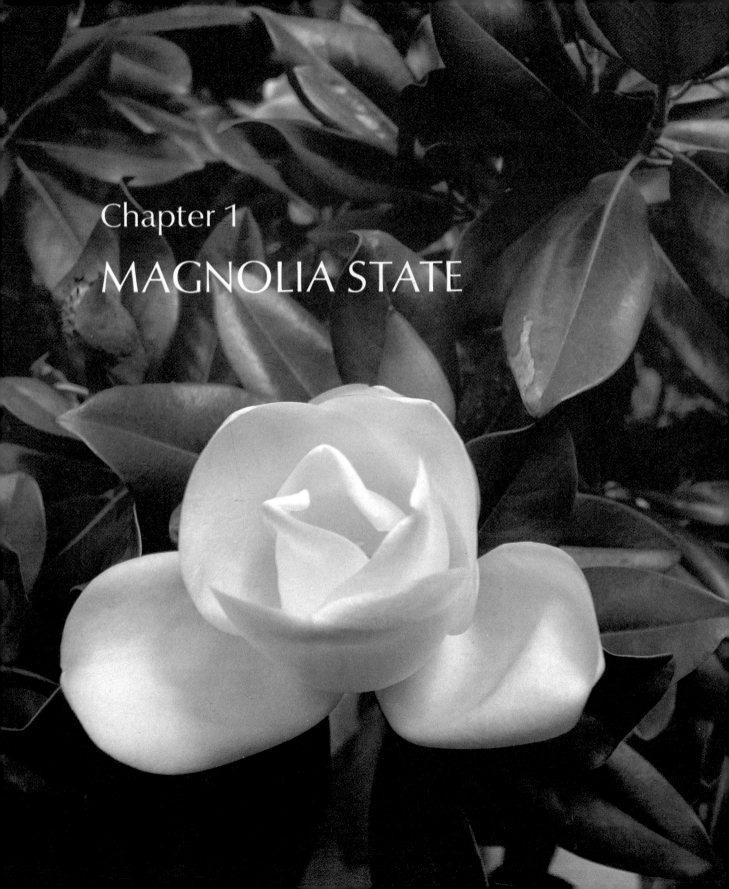

Chapter 1
MAGNOLIA STATE

MAGNOLIA STATE

Early in 1988, Mississippi's recently elected governor, Ray Mabus, Jr., observed that in a sense Mississippi was the "newest of the fifty states." None had changed more in so short a time and none, he predicted, would change more rapidly and dramatically in the future.

Mississippi has had serious handicaps to overcome. At the start of this century, it appeared that the state lacked the proper resources to compete in an industrial world. Mississippi seemed bound by old ways, overly dependent on the uncertainties of farming. The state lacked a skilled work force and many of its promising young people were moving to more prosperous states.

Since that time, Mississippi has taken giant steps forward. It is indeed a "new state," yet it has managed to preserve much of its rich heritage.

The magnolia is the state tree and the magnolia blossom is the state flower. They are appropriate symbols, for the beautiful trees thrive almost anywhere in Mississippi. The blossoms are not merely the delicate blossoms of old plantations. Magnolias are tough. Their strong roots search the earth for water; the silvery blue-green leaves look soft at a glance but are strong and leathery to the touch.

Mississippians, too, have managed on soil that was not always fertile. They have known harsh conflicts and great change. The blossoming of modern Mississippi is a remarkable story of promise and success that is still unfolding.

Chapter 2
THE LAND

THE LAND

Today, a traveler crossing Mississippi on its main highways sees a tamed and settled land dotted by old towns and mellowing farms. Dairy herds graze serenely and seem to be a part of the eternal scenery.

Despite appearances, some wilderness is never far away in Mississippi. Pine trees in the distance hint that—even today—about half of Mississippi's land is covered with forest. Stretches of marsh or woodland remind us that much of this land was once a region of swamps and tangled thickets. With only a little imagination, a visitor can see Choctaw and Chickasaw Indian hunters move on moccasined feet along hidden game trails.

Even in its wilds, Mississippi has always offered beauty and promise. Travelers have always felt welcomed by its sunlight, by the fragrance and gentleness of its air.

GEOGRAPHY AND TOPOGRAPHY

Mississippi, in the Deep South, is medium sized. Its area of 47,716 square miles (123,583 square kilometers) places it thirty-second in area among the fifty states. Alabama lies immediately to its east, Tennessee to the north, and Arkansas and Louisiana to the west. The twisty western border resembles a piece of a jigsaw puzzle. Shaped by the ever-changing Mississippi River, the border has loops, points, and curlicues. The western boundary of the state may change from day to day. A bit of land that was part of

The bald cypress trees lining the banks of the Pascagoula River (left)
and the wooded areas along the Chunky River (right) are reminders that
much of Mississippi was once a region of swamps and tangled thickets.

Mississippi yesterday may be part of Arkansas or Louisiana next
month. The land has not moved, but the river has.

To the south, Mississippi borders a corner of Louisiana, but 44
miles (71 kilometers) of coastline along the Gulf of Mexico form
most of the state's southern border. This coastline is the lowest
point in the state, sea level. The highest crest is Woodall Mountain
at Iuka, rising 806 feet (246 meters).

Mississippi has two main regions, the Alluvial Plain and the
East Gulf Coastal Plain. Each has its own distinct soil, resources,
and character. The two regions and their differences have had a
powerful effect in shaping the history and lives of Mississippi's
people.

THE ALLUVIAL PLAIN: GIFT OF RIVERS

Thousands upon thousands of years ago, the Ohio River flowed
far south of its present course, ultimately pouring into the
Mississippi River near what is now Greenville, Mississippi. Other

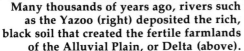
Many thousands of years ago, rivers such as the Yazoo (right) deposited the rich, black soil that created the fertile farmlands of the Alluvial Plain, or Delta (above).

rivers, the Yazoo in particular, also converged near this point, forming a gigantic meeting of waters.

The rivers carried rich, black soil from upstream. When the rivers receded after a flood, and as they changed courses, they left behind deposits of this rich soil. These deposits are called "alluvial" because they came from rivers. Over the ages, these deposits created the Alluvial Plain, which extends along the entire western border of the state. Mississippians call this region the Delta. In the northwest corner of the state, the Delta provides the richest soil in the South. The Delta remained tangled woods and swamps until the 1850s. Then slowly its wealth and power grew until Delta planters virtually dominated the state.

The southern section of the Delta, a narrow strip of land edging the Mississippi River banks, is called the River Lowlands. It was once called the Natchez District for its largest city. The River Lowlands are part of the Alluvial Plain, yet are different. Here the first European planters—with their African slaves—began farming. Their early wealth built great mansions much admired today. But the river rose in terrible floods, cotton exhausted the soil, and erosion became a serious problem. The region, while rich in history, has lost much in population and prosperity.

THE EAST GULF COASTAL PLAIN

The broad East Gulf Coastal Plain includes all of Mississippi east of the Alluvial Plain. Most of the Old Natchez District is in this region. Unlike the Delta, where various counties resemble each other, the Coastal Plain is a patchwork of regions. Much of the varied, often broken, country is hilly and pine-clad and crisscrossed by streams and low ridges. Early farms in this region tended to be small. Here are the Piney Woods, the forested Flatwoods, and the Hills.

Shortly before the Civil War, cotton plantations spread from the Delta over part of the Coastal Plain. But this demanding crop soon depleted the thin soil. The plantations were broken into smaller farms, some raising crops, others raising dairy cattle. But these hills and prairies seldom supported good farming for long, and life on these farms was often difficult and taxing.

In northeastern Mississippi, the Black Prairie, or Black Belt, named for its dark soil, reaches into the state like a giant finger. This is cattle, corn, and cotton country.

At the southern tip of the Coastal Plain lies the sandy Gulf Coast, a world of its own, attracting tourists to its warm beaches.

THE BIG RIVER, FRIEND AND ENEMY

The Mississippi River, whose name in Choctaw means "Father of Waters," is the backbone of the United States. The Mississippi is the world's third-longest river (2,348 miles/3,779 kilometers) and drains a basin that is one-third the area of the United States.

The river, crowded with steamboats, was America's greatest highway in the 1800s. River commerce, as much as agriculture, enriched such lovely Mississippi River ports as Natchez,

Vicksburg, and Greenville. Even today, the Mississippi is the nation's greatest inland waterway.

Greenville, one of the state's largest riverfront cities, has known both the river's generosity and its danger. Many times the angry river snatched away whole blocks and neighborhoods of Greenville. In 1927, for instance, a flood left the entire town under water for seventy days!

That same 1927 rampage of the river caused nearly two hundred thousand Mississippians to flee and cost one hundred thousand people their homes. The terrible losses of life and property spurred vigorous efforts at flood control. The state built new levees, or dikes, along the river to hold back floodwaters. At Greenville, the Mississippi was forced into a channel six miles (ten kilometers) west of the town, leaving a lake for a port. Greenville was safe at last, and so were farms and other Mississippi towns along the river.

OTHER RIVER WATER

The Yazoo and the Big Black are the main rivers that flow through the state and empty into the Mississippi. Three of the state's important rivers empty directly into the Gulf of Mexico: the Pearl, the Pascagoula, and the Tombigbee. In addition to its many rivers, Mississippi has many bayous—slow-moving bodies of water that eventually feed into the rivers.

The largest lakes are reservoirs, artificially made, long, narrow lakes formed by flood-control dams. The Grenada Reservoir, near Grenada, covers 64,000 acres (25,900 hectares). Other reservoir lakes in the Delta region are the Arkabutla, Enid, and Sardis. Pickwick Lake is a large reservoir in the northeast corner of the state. The Ross Barnett Reservoir, on the Pearl River above

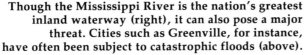

Though the Mississippi River is the nation's greatest
inland waterway (right), it can also pose a major
threat. Cities such as Greenville, for instance,
have often been subject to catastrophic floods (above).

Jackson, provides water and recreation for the state's largest city.
When the Mississippi River has abruptly changed course, it has
left behind "oxbow lakes," named for their shape. Beulah Lake
and Moon Lake are two oxbow lakes made by the river.

CLIMATE

Mississippi enjoys a mild climate, with warm summers and
gentle winters. The balmy south is usually frost-free for a season
of 250 to 300 days. July temperatures average 82 degrees
Fahrenheit (28 degrees Celsius). In January, the thermometer
stands at an average of 48 degrees Fahrenheit (9 degrees Celsius).

Precipitation is almost entirely rain and ranges from 50 inches
(127 centimeters) in the northwest to 65 inches (165 centimeters)
in the moist southeast. There is occasional snow or sleet in the
northern part of the state.

There are dramatic exceptions to the rule of a mild climate.
Hurricanes have surged north from the Gulf of Mexico, pounding
the Mississippi coast with devastating force.

In the spring and summer, redbuds (left), camellias, and azaleas (above) brighten Mississippi gardens, parks, and roadsides.

One of the state's worst was Hurricane Camille, with winds of 172 miles (277 kilometers) per hour. Camille roared in on August 17, 1969. The winds picked up automobiles and turned them upside down like toys, snapped tree trunks as if they were toothpicks, and flattened crops like a steamroller. Wind-driven waves rolled across the coastal highway and destroyed oceanside businesses and homes. Fortunately, severe hurricanes are relatively rare.

In 1971, two years after Camille struck, Mississippi was hit by a spate of tornadoes that took more than a hundred lives and caused millions of dollars in damage. Tornadoes pose their greatest threat to the state during the spring and the fall.

MISSISSIPPI OUTDOORS

Climate, soil, and the modern conservation of forests have contributed to the abundance of plant and animal life in

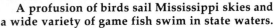
A profusion of birds sail Mississippi skies and a wide variety of game fish swim in state waters.

Mississippi. Deer and smaller animals such as rabbits, squirrels, foxes, opossums, and even beavers thrive in the lush wildlife areas. A fascinating profusion of birds, including wild doves, ducks, quail, and mockingbirds sail the sky. Mississippi catfish are famous, as are the state's bass, bream, and crappies. Deep-sea fishermen test their luck along the Gulf Coast, where crab, shrimp, oysters, mackerel, and speckled trout are found.

Pines of several varieties are the most common trees, but cottonwood, hickory, cedar, elm, and oak trees shade houses and tower in the woods. Five trees especially typical of Mississippi are the pecan, sweet gum, bald cypress, and tupelo, as well as the beautiful magnolia.

Mississippians take pride in their flowers. Gardeners vie to grow the loveliest azaleas and camellias. In the spring and the summer, the fields are sprinkled with black-eyed Susans, crepe myrtle, dogwood, camellias, redbud, and violets. Pink and white Cherokee roses make a fragrant Mississippi bouquet.

17

Chapter 3
THE PEOPLE

THE PEOPLE

The United States Census revealed that in 1990, Mississippi had a population of 2,573,216. It is the thirty-first most-populous state. Nearly all of its people (99 percent) were born in the United States and the vast majority (80 percent) were born in Mississippi, as were their parents and even their grandparents.

In the United States, where there is so much movement and travel, it is unusual to find so many people living in the same state where their ancestors were born. This continuity has given Mississippians strong feelings of heritage and tradition.

The majority of the white farmers who settled Mississippi were descended from Northern Europeans, mostly from the British Isles. In the 1700s, many of the original settlers, especially those in the northeastern counties of the state, came directly overland from Virginia and the Carolinas. They brought with them their beliefs, customs, and traditions. Because transportation was often slow and difficult, many of the new communities were isolated. People preserved their customary ways.

Some settlers of the 1700s and 1800s brought with them, or soon imported, African slaves. Most of the slaves were natives of West Africa, where there were large slave markets. Even today, descendants of these two groups make up the majority of Mississippi's population.

Of Mississippians who belong to a church, more than half are Baptists and a fourth are Methodists. There are also many Roman

Though more than three-quarters of churchgoing Mississippians are Baptists or Methodists, many others are Roman Catholics, Presbyterians, or Episcopalians.

Catholics, Presbyterians, and Episcopalians. Most of the Jewish population is concentrated in several cities, among them Meridian, Greenville, Clarksdale, and Jackson.

MIGRATION AND IMMIGRATION

The 1990 census showed that 36 percent of the population, or about one of every three Mississippians, is black. No other state has such a large proportion of black citizens; yet there were times when blacks outnumbered whites. The change is due to both migration and immigration trends.

Even though the state's economy is no longer based primarily on agriculture, farming provides an income for many Mississippians.

For the last hundred years, more people have moved away from Mississippi than have moved to the state. Difficult farming conditions drove many to seek better jobs and greater opportunity in big cities. But the state lacked such industrial centers. Further, many young people, especially blacks, were impatient with the state's slow-to-change society and customs. As people left the state, the ratio of blacks to whites decreased.

An era of progress began in the late 1960s and early 1970s. Mississippi has created new opportunities in jobs, education, the arts, and politics. The state is making a determined effort to hold onto its most precious resource, its young people. And the waves of migration seem to be lessening.

Even while these migrations took place, immigration was changing the population of Mississippi. In the late 1860s, Delta plantation owners brought in a number of Chinese laborers. Today, Mississippi has more Chinese Americans than any other southern state. Italian Americans, Greek Americans, and Yugoslav

Most Mississippians still live in close-knit, long-settled towns and counties, even though the state is becoming more and more industrialized.

Americans are scattered through the state, with some concentration on the Gulf Coast. Descendants of French settlers live in the southwest. Mississippians of French or Yugoslav descent are prominent in the state's fishing industry. More recent arrivals have been immigrants from Latin America and Asia, predominantly from Vietnam.

All these groups have made contributions to Mississippi's culture and economy. Yet they make up only 1 percent of the population.

POPULATION DISTRIBUTION AND MIGRATION

"Here in Mississippi," said a woman from Laurel, "everybody knows everybody else, or at least knows who their cousins are."

In a state of two and a half million people this, of course, cannot be literally true. Yet it gives an idea of how many Mississippians feel about their close-knit, long-settled towns and counties. Most Mississippians live on farms or in small towns. As a rule, the same

Biloxi, one of the state's chief gulf ports, is Mississippi's second-largest city.

families lived in a town for generation after generation. Everyone knew all their neighbors, and the arrival of a stranger was rare and noticeable.

This pattern of rural life, with the population spread rather evenly across the state, lasted more than a century. In the early 1940s, the mechanization of agriculture began to force farm workers off the farms and toward towns and cities in search of jobs. Cities began to grow and industry came to Mississippi. Now, nearly 47 percent of the people live in cities while 53 percent of the people live in rural areas. Even the rural areas have changed. Originally, most rural dwellers lived on farms, but that is no longer true in Mississippi. Today, only 20 percent of the population lives on farms.

The state capital, Jackson, is Mississippi's largest city. The five next largest, in order of population, are Biloxi, Greenville, Hattiesburg, Meridian, and Gulfport. Three cities—Greenville, Natchez, and Vicksburg—stand on the banks of the Mississippi and flourish as river ports.

POLITICS AND REGIONALISM

For many decades after the Civil War, plantation owners of the rich Delta region controlled Mississippi politics and dominated the poorer white farmers who worked the less-fertile land called the Hills. The same politicians were elected over and over again to offices in the state capital and in Washington, D.C. Except for a brief time during Reconstruction, blacks were not allowed to vote effectively and held no offices. Politically, Mississippi was part of the "Solid South" or "Deep South," meaning it voted so solidly for the Democratic party that there was no other contest.

As new industry came to Mississippi, the power of the Delta planters weakened. The national Voting Rights Act of 1965 and subsequent changes in state laws permitted blacks to vote and have those votes be meaningful.

Black leaders have now become an important force in Mississippi politics, and the one-party system has been broken. Mississippi voters have chosen Democrats, Republicans, and Independent candidates. The "solid" vote is gone forever, and the people of Mississippi have shown that no one can be sure of what they may decide in an election.

Chapter 4
THE BEGINNING

THE BEGINNING

The distant past is as shadowy as the woodlands of Mississippi. But it seems that about twelve thousand years ago, hunting peoples were already living on the land. The people were wanderers who followed game and depended on animals for food and clothing. They left behind only a few clues about themselves—some tools, weapons, and bones.

As centuries passed, the early Mississippians gathered shellfish, nuts, berries, and wild plants for food, but they still depended heavily on hunting and fishing. They built huts of poles and branches, tanned animal skins, and wove baskets. These ancient Mississippians traded their goods for copper ornaments and tools that were made by other Indian groups. Some of these items came from as far north as Lake Michigan. Even then, the Mississippi River was important for trade.

Knowledge of agriculture existed in the Mississippi Valley more than three thousand years ago. By 800 B.C., Indian farmers were cultivating the cornlike maize that had been first domesticated from wild plants in Mexico. Squash, beans, and tobacco were also grown. The people were now able to live in villages near their fields and no longer needed to wander after game for food. Some time after these early people began to live in permanent communities, they began to make pottery and other clay utensils.

About A.D. 1000, new discoveries and ideas seem to have spread south from people living in the northern Mississippi Valley. The

Emerald Mound, near Natchez (left), was built about A.D. 1000. A Natchez house and corn granary (above) have been reconstructed at the original site of the Grand Village of the Natchez Indians, in Natchez.

people built flat-topped mounds somewhat like pyramids and erected temples on them. These man-made hills are unlike Indian mounds in other parts of the United States. The Mississippi mounds were not burial places, but shrines for worship of the sun. Remains of these Native-American structures can still be seen in Mississippi, most notably near Greenville and Natchez.

When Europeans arrived in Mississippi, there were various native peoples in the region, but the dominant groups were Choctaw, Chickasaw, and Natchez.

The Natchez, perhaps direct descendants of the earlier temple builders, had developed a complex and highly organized society, including organized religion and a system of government that resembled a monarchy.

Different from the Natchez but similar to each other were the Choctaw and Chickasaw peoples. They shared many religious beliefs and their languages were related. Both groups had established democratic forms of government and enjoyed a large measure of individual freedom.

In 1541, Spanish explorer Hernando De Soto led an expedition through what are now the states of Florida, Georgia, Alabama, Mississippi, and Arkansas. During their unsuccessful search for gold and riches, De Soto and his party became the first Europeans to reach the Mississippi River (left).

EUROPEANS COME TO MISSISSIPPI

In 1541, eighty years before the Pilgrims landed at Plymouth Rock, Spaniards seeking gold came to Mississippi. These Spaniards left empty-handed after their leader, Hernando De Soto, died. Their sojourn was hardly more than a ripple on the Great River.

In 1682, French explorer René-Robert Cavelier, Sieur de La Salle, came down the Mississippi River from Canada. Although he saw little more than the riverbanks, he boldly claimed the vast Mississippi Valley for France. La Salle named the region Louisiana in honor of King Louis XIV. The present state of Mississippi was part of this sweeping claim.

In 1699, the French founded a settlement, Fort Maurepas, at what is now Ocean Springs. They built Fort Rosalie in 1716, at the site of modern Natchez. Meanwhile, English traders had begun to barter with the Chickasaws in 1698. Always at the edge of the scene were Spaniards in Florida and Mexico watching for opportunities to capture the land.

The European traders brought valuable goods to Mississippi, including metal knives and axes. They also brought domestic animals such as horses, cows, and pigs. All of these seemed marvelous and wonderful to the native peoples. Unfortunately, the Europeans also brought diseases, war, and an intense greed for land. The native civilizations, which had served their people well, were doomed before this foreign onslaught.

French colonists imported the first black African slaves in 1719. Slave labor was quickly put to use on the region's rice and tobacco plantations.

John Law, a crafty Scottish adventurer who was appointed treasurer to the French crown, promoted a scheme to enrich himself and many investors. He lured colonists to the area with false promises. The advertising did attract settlers, but his plan only lost money.

The French claim to huge North American territories was challenged by the British, who allied themselves with the Chickasaws. Together, the British and the Chickasaws kept France from extending her power. At last France gave up the struggle, and in 1763, the British flag flew over the land east of the Mississippi River. Until 1779, Britain ruled an area that included the coastal regions of Mississippi and Alabama (West Florida) and an area including the Florida panhandle (East Florida).

MISSISSIPPI BECOMES AMERICAN

In the 1770s, events along the faraway Atlantic coast were shaping Mississippi's future. The thirteen British colonies rose in the revolt called the American Revolution.

Spain saw the war as a chance to seize the British provinces of West and East Florida. Again the flag flying over what is now

During the years when Spain had control over Mississippi, this house in Natchez, called Bontura, belonged to the Spanish rulers.

Mississippi changed: it was now Spanish. But Spain's rule, like Britain's before that, lasted only sixteen years. When the victorious Americans established a new nation, it was clear that Spain could not hold all the Florida territories. Most of the province passed to the United States in a treaty of 1795, although the Spanish clung to the seacoast.

In 1798, the United States Congress organized the Mississippi Territory. It was a long belt of land stretching from the Mississippi River to the Chattahoochee River on the western Georgia border. It did not reach as far south as the Gulf of Mexico, but included more than half of what is now Mississippi. The entire northern part remained under Indian control.

The young territory faced many problems. Its borders were disputed. Claims to land had become clouded after so many changes of government. The few "roads" were barely passable trails, and there was no access to the sea except overland through regions controlled by Spain to the south and France to the west in Louisiana.

The first territorial governor, Winthrop Sargent, was appointed by President John Adams. The territorial capital was established at Natchez. Sargent struggled to organize a government out of the

Much of the original Natchez Trace was a narrow path that followed routes long used by the Indians.

territorial confusion. His successor, William C. C. Claiborne, continued this work and was able to settle many of the tangled land claims.

THE NATCHEZ TRACE

In the early days, it was easy enough to get from the North to the Mississippi Territory. Boatmen just floated down the Mississippi River to Natchez. But how could they get back? Traveling against the river's current was difficult at any time; it was impossible part of the year.

In 1801, Choctaw and Chickasaw representatives gave the United States permission to build a road from Nashville, Tennessee to Natchez, Mississippi. This created the Natchez Trace, meaning trail. Much of the Trace was only a narrow path that followed routes that had long been used by the Indians.

The Trace attracted many travelers. And so it also attracted robbers who hid in the forests and swamps to sally forth and prey on travelers. The Mason-Harpe boys were the most infamous of these highwaymen. Governor Claiborne posted a reward of $2,000 for their capture. Eventually, the criminals came to violent ends.

AMERICA EXPANDS

The 1803 Louisiana Purchase made the Mississippi River an American waterway. The Mississippi Territory now had access to the Gulf of Mexico and was ripe for growth. Bits and pieces of surrounding land were incorporated into the territory. Land north to the Tennessee border became part of the territory. But Spain still held the Gulf Coast, and along that border there was conflict between Spanish officials and the settlers.

These problems exploded into violence in 1810. About one hundred settlers took control of the West Florida region along the coast and captured the Spanish fort at Baton Rouge. A month later, President James Madison sent forces to occupy all of Spanish West Florida except Mobile. In 1812, that part of West Florida east of the Pearl River was added to the Mississippi Territory.

When war between the United States and Britain broke out in 1812, Mississippians were quickly called upon to defend their land. Many of the Mississippians were Choctaw and Chickasaw Indians. The Choctaw helped General Andrew Jackson crush an uprising of Creek Indians and to defeat the British in the Battle of New Orleans. Nearly a thousand Choctaw warriors fought under Jackson and helped win a great victory.

At the end of the war, white settlers came to the Mississippi Territory and brought or imported more African slaves. In less than twenty years, Mississippi had changed from an isolated, landlocked, and often lawless region into a thriving land. People were even beginning to talk of statehood, a dream that was indeed only two years away.

Chapter 5

PIONEER CONQUEST

PIONEER CONQUEST

On December 10, 1817, Mississippi was admitted to the Union as the twentieth state. The Mississippi Territory had been divided into the new state, with boundaries much as they are today, and the Alabama Territory. Mississippi was now a state, but the land remained rough and rugged. So many bears still roamed the forests and wandered into farmyards that bear grease and bear fur remained important products. One traveler reported that Mississippi had the most "terrific murders" and "gorgeous bank robberies" in the world. As for the Indians, whites were "stealing their land by the township."

There were twenty-five thousand whites and twenty-three thousand black slaves plus a few free blacks in Mississippi on the eve of statehood. No one counted the Indian population. However, today's historians estimate that about thirty-five thousand Indians lived in the region as white exploration and settlement began. More than half the whites and three-fourths of the slaves lived in the old Natchez area. This small strip of land had the best water transportation in all the state. The rest of the people were scattered throughout the wilderness. Indians held two-thirds of the land.

Mississippi in those days had little resemblance to the Old South of stately white-columned mansions. It was the frontier — rather like the Wild West that Americans would know later, rife with bandits, gunfighters, and buckskin-clad hunters and trappers.

REMOVAL OF THE NATIVE PEOPLES

White settlers eager for land arrived daily by river, by sea, and down the Natchez Trace. Where better to get land than from the Indians who held the central and northern areas of the state? Why, the settlers asked, should Indians control more land than they farmed? There was little understanding of Indian customs and no respect for Indian culture. Some white Mississippians regarded the Native Americans as an inferior race to be driven away. Others tried to protect the rights of the Indians, but with little success.

Indian land was taken through bribery and trickery, under pretext of debts, and by outright seizure. The scheme of the United States was to move and relocate the native peoples far to the west in Indian Territory, which is now the state of Oklahoma.

The fate of the Choctaw was typical of many Indian nations. After great pressure, the Choctaw signed a treaty at Dancing Rabbit Creek in 1830: they would trade their Mississippi land for land in little-known Oklahoma. By 1832, many of the Chocktaw had left Mississippi. The fate of those remaining was to be determined by events in the East.

Representatives of the Cherokee had ceded Indian lands to Georgia. The treaty was appealed to the United States Supreme Court. Although the treaty was declared invalid, Georgia officials continued with the Indian removal. The Cherokee were forced to march from Georgia to the Indian Territory. As the march moved westward, Choctaw and Chickasaw Indians remaining in Mississippi were forced to join the march. Few marchers survived. Many fell to hunger, many to a terrible blizzard, and finally, others fell to a cholera plague. This forced march is known as the Trail of Tears.

Several thousand Choctaw still make their homes on Indian land near Philadelphia, in the east-central part of the state.

A few Chickasaw and Choctaw managed to stay in Mississippi for generations, enduring hard lives. About 6,100 Indians live in Mississippi today. There is a small Choctaw reservation in east-central Mississippi, the last of the once-vast Indian lands. It consists of seven separate pieces of land totaling only twenty-seven square miles (seventy square kilometers).

GROWTH

The opening of Indian lands to white settlement brought a tide of immigration. Mississippi's future United States senator, Robert Walker, rejoiced: "Kentucky's coming, Tennessee's coming, Alabama's coming, and they're all coming to join the joyous crowd of Mississippians."

The population now reached beyond the Natchez area and spread across the state. A capital in a more central location was needed. The village of Le Fleur's Bluff on the Pearl River was chosen. The site was renamed Jackson, and in 1822, slaves began to lay bricks for a new capitol building. Mississippians wanted

Because communities on the Mississippi River had natural transportation for their goods, they had little interest in road building.

their capital to be a good-sized city, so they lured immigrants to the areas surrounding Jackson by promising land. To acquire a farm, all a man had to do was promise to build a house on it.

The state was booming. In the ten years between 1830 and 1840, the population almost tripled, increasing from about 137,000 to nearly 376,000.

Growth brought problems. For instance, the building of roads did not keep pace with the founding of towns. Part of the reason was political: communities on the rivers dominated the state, and they already had fine natural transportation—by water. So these powerful communities had little interest in road building.

Land sold for $1.25 an acre when the scramble began, but it soon grew expensive. Slaves to work the land were also costly. Mississippi was developing a rich class, the plantation owners. A much poorer class tilled small farms, raised cattle, or worked at lumbering. Despite its growing pains, Mississippi was rapidly becoming one of the richest states of that time.

Plantation owners and farmers bought black slaves at auctions or slave markets such as this one.

SLAVERY AND PLANTATION LIFE

The majority of whites in Mississippi did not own slaves. In general, it was the large plantations and some of the smaller farms that depended on slave labor. A few blacks were town slaves, working in towns for owners who used them as blacksmiths and carpenters, or in larger cities, as factory and mill hands.

House slaves worked at tasks usually performed by servants. These slaves were often better fed, clothed, and educated than those who toiled at farming. House slaves were well treated by their owners and often cared for the owner's children.

Field slaves worked from sunrise to sunset, pausing only at midday for lunch and a brief rest. In winter, they made repairs on the plantation or were rented out as woodcutters, fence builders, railroad laborers, or factory workers.

Slave owners had complete power over their slaves. An owner could punish slaves, perhaps by cruel whippings. He could

Field slaves at work on a Mississippi River cotton plantation

overwork them, insisting they work even when they were sick or injured. An owner could even break up families by selling family members to other owners.

Slave owners lived in constant fear of slave rebellions. Any hint of rebellion or disorder was quickly and violently suppressed. Slave codes were stern. Reading and writing were forbidden. Slaves were not permitted to defend themselves physically against whites, nor could they testify against whites in courts of law.

Many whites in the slave-owning society were aware of the evils of slavery but could not think of a way to end it. They could not imagine a world different from the one they already knew.

MISSISSIPPI FARMS

Plantation owners, of course, had far easier and more secure lives than the slaves. But the Mississippian's world was not all shady porches, fans, and cool drinks. Most Mississippi white women married young and had many children. These women worked hard at cooking, butchering, making soap, sewing clothes,

Most Mississippians lived simply and worked hard for a living. Even those who had slaves labored in the home and the fields beside them.

and drying vegetables and fruits to preserve them. Most white farmers labored in the fields from dawn to dusk. Even if a farmer owned a slave or two, he labored in the fields beside them.

The typical Mississippi farmhouse of the time was not like the great mansions found today at Natchez and other cities. More likely a farmer lived in a two-room log house, his children sleeping in a loft under the roof. His wife cooked daily at a big, smoky fireplace and did the laundry outside, working at a big iron pot over an open fire. Life in this pioneer world meant hard work and long hours for almost everybody.

KING COTTON

The wealth of the young state of Mississippi came chiefly from a single crop: cotton. In 1793, Eli Whitney invented the cotton gin, a machine that could clean cotton as fast as fifty people working by hand. A black farmer named Barclay was shown a rough sketch of Whitney's device in 1795 and built Mississippi's first cotton gin. About a dozen years later, another boon fell to Mississippi cotton

The cotton gin (above) helped speed up one of the steps in preparing cotton for market, but tasks such as pressing cotton into bales (left) also required hard work and many hands.

growers. An improved cottonseed had been developed from seeds from Mexico. The new seed helped to further increase the production of cotton.

Cotton rapidly became America's most valuable export. In 1830, Mississippi was perhaps the greatest cotton-growing area in the world. The state produced a record crop of 387,000 bales, more than any other state. At harvest time, the steamboats on Mississippi's main rivers were piled so high with cotton bales that only the boats' smokestacks were visible.

Mississipians boasted that the world could not get along without cotton from the American South. They looked on "King Cotton" as a never-ending source of wealth and power. It would be a while before they had to admit that this king was an unpredictable tyrant.

In the mid-1800s, no one suspected the crop's unreliability. Mississippians rode the crest of cotton prosperity. In the 1850s, Irish immigrants and slave gangs toiled to build higher levees and to drain Delta swamps—all to help Mississippi cotton become the richest crop in the land.

Meanwhile, a storm was gathering—the Civil War that would sweep through the cotton kingdom more powerfully than any flood and change the old ways forever.

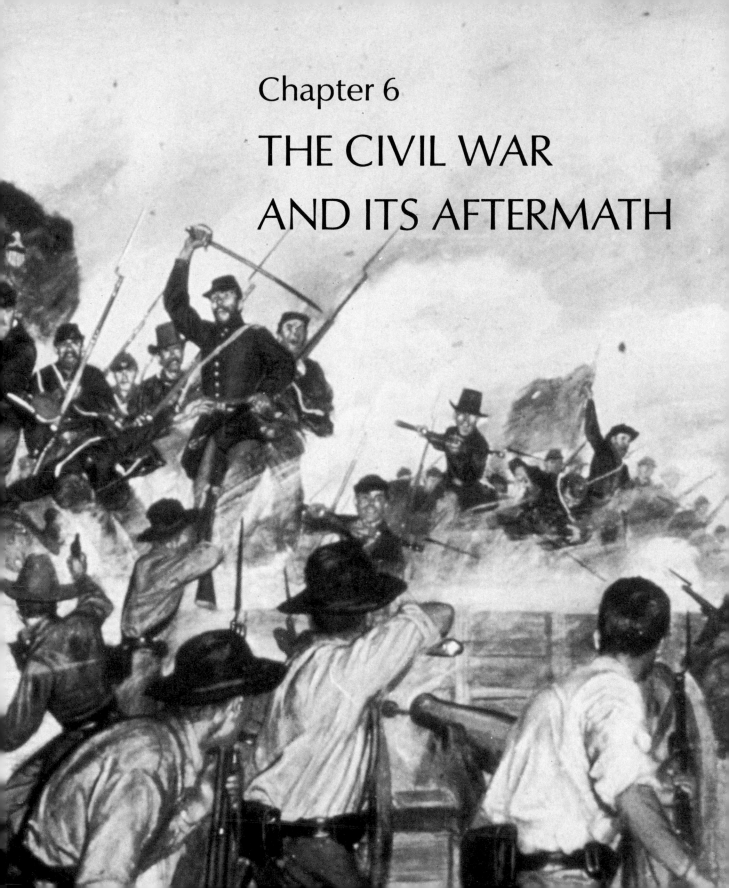

Chapter 6

THE CIVIL WAR
AND ITS AFTERMATH

THE CIVIL WAR AND ITS AFTERMATH

On January 9, 1861, bells pealed and brass bands played rousing music in Jackson, Mississippi. A glittering parade marched down the street past the capitol. A silken flag fluttered at the head of the parade. The flag was not the familiar stars and stripes; instead, the cheering throngs were saluting a blue banner with a single white star, a banner of Mississippi. The parade celebrated the state's secession, its withdrawal from the United States.

The leaders of the state had just participated in an emotional convention that addressed the question of secession. In angry debates, some leaders pleaded to keep Mississippi in the Union, or, at the very least, submit the question to a direct vote of the people. A group called "fire-eaters," zealots long dedicated to slavery and an independent Mississippi, argued for secession. The vote to separate from the Union was eighty-four to fifteen. "Mississippi is out!" trumpeted a state newspaper.

Seldom has a venture doomed to pain, death, and ruin been welcomed so joyfully. Soon, seventy-eight thousand white sons of Mississippi would be wearing the gray uniform of the Confederate army. More than a third of them would be killed or wounded. But in early 1861, honor and glory were celebrated; few people thought of death and ruin.

TROUBLE BOILS OVER

The crisis had been brewing for a long time. There had been years of disputes between the northern and southern states. Crisis after crisis had been resolved. In 1832 and again in 1851, Mississippians had refused to join attempts to leave the Union. But powerful slave owners in the southern states felt more and more that their way of life was being threatened. Then, Abraham Lincoln was elected president in 1860. Because Lincoln had spoken against slavery, worry changed to outright fear and anger. Secession fever swept the South. When South Carolina withdrew from the Union, Mississippi immediately followed, quickly joining the Confederate States of America.

The people of Mississippi were not asked through a ballot if they wanted to leave the United States. The majority of Mississippians were slaves and had no vote. Many whites, especially small farmers in the Piney Woods and Tennessee Hills, opposed secession. Doubtless the fire-eaters would have won a vote on withdrawal, but the state was far from united.

There was also a wide belief that no war would follow secession. Yet many people seemed to welcome war, claiming that the South would win quickly and easily.

Jefferson Davis, Mississippi's leading statesman, had few such illusions. Born in Kentucky but raised in Mississippi, Davis had served in Congress and had been secretary of war. In 1860, he was a United States senator from Mississippi. He believed in a state's right to secede but argued against it, fearing that secession would bring armed conflict. Davis, soon to become the president of the Confederate States of America, warned all the South to prepare for a terrible struggle. "A war . . . the like of which men have not seen," was how he described what he foresaw.

Jefferson Davis (left), president of the Confederate States of America, spent his last years at Beauvoir, his Biloxi home (above).

MISSISSIPPI GOES TO WAR

Mississippi held a vital position in the Civil War. Whoever controlled the state, controlled traffic on the great river. If the North captured the river, the Confederacy would be cut in two and important transportation would be halted. Northern generals made plans to accomplish exactly that.

Early in the war, Mississippians rejoiced at news of southern victories in the East. Yet almost from the beginning, military affairs went badly on their own doorstep.

Mississippi imported most of the factory-made goods it used. It depended on its cotton to provide money for these goods. When export was halted by the federal naval blockade, the cotton piled up in warehouses. The state could not ship the cotton and so would lose the revenue the crop might bring. Worse, although the state was a great cotton producer, it did not have mills to make cotton into cloth. Except for a few small factories in the western part of the state, there were no industries to make weapons or other tools of war. Northern warships were choking Mississippi.

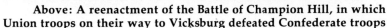
Above: A reenactment of the Battle of Champion Hill, in which Union troops on their way to Vicksburg defeated Confederate troops

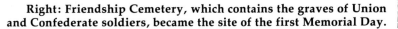
Right: Friendship Cemetery, which contains the graves of Union and Confederate soldiers, became the site of the first Memorial Day.

A major transportation center for the South was the town of Corinth, in northeastern Mississippi. Several railroads met at Corinth. The fierce Battle of Shiloh was fought just north of Corinth in Tennessee. About fifty-two thousand Confederate soldiers faced more than sixty thousand Union soldiers. After two days of fierce fighting, Confederate forces retreated from Shiloh to Corinth. A month later, the Confederate army was forced to abandon the railroad town. In a way, Shiloh was a battle without a victory; thirteen thousand Union soldiers and more than ten thousand Confederate soldiers died. Mississippi now knew the bitterness of war.

Vicksburg, a Mississippi River port and rail center, became the next target for Union general Ulysses S. Grant. The struggle for the city is a landmark in American history. After heavy military action on both sides of the Mississippi River, Vicksburg was tightly surrounded by General Grant's forces. Many of the townspeople dug caves or fled to cellars to escape heavy shelling from land-based cannons as well as from gunboats on the river. Weeks went by and food became desperately short. Some people considered themselves lucky to have mule meat to eat. An army officer reported that the tension of the siege was so terrible that soon the inhabitants might become "maniacs."

Despite this dire report, the townspeople stayed surprisingly calm and cheerful in the beleaguered city. A newspaper managed to keep publishing through the entire siege.

Vicksburg finally surrendered to Union forces on July 4, 1863, after withstanding forty-seven days of pressure such as no American city had ever faced. The Mississippi River, despite stubborn southern resistance, was in northern hands. The war had reached a major turning point.

The fall of Vicksburg was followed by other battles and great destruction in Mississippi, but the decisive military action had ended.

THE END OF SLAVERY

On New Year's Day, 1863, President Lincoln declared in the Emancipation Proclamation that slaves were free, but well before that time, the Union army had been freeing slaves. Throughout the war, the Union army was aided by Mississippi slaves who acted as guides and spies in hopes of gaining their freedom. More than seventeen thousand black Mississippians served in the Union army, working as scouts, blacksmiths, and cooks long before they were used as combat soldiers.

As the war ground to an end, thousands of slaves claimed their freedom, following the victorious Union army across the state. Blacks hailed 1864 as the "jubilee year," the beginning of freedom for four hundred thousand slaves in Mississippi.

When the Confederate army surrendered in the spring of 1865, the people of Mississippi found themselves in the midst of chaos and hardship. Railroads had been destroyed, levees were in

To get his army into position to take Vicksburg, Union General Ulysses Grant ran his gunboats past the Confederate gun batteries on the bluffs of the Mississippi River (top left). The USS *Cairo* (above) had been sunk in an earlier attempt to clear Confederate batteries north of Vicksburg.

During the siege, many townspeople lived in caves to escape the heavy shelling (left).

After the surrender, the Union forces marched in and took possession of the city (below).

Vicksburg National Military Park (bottom left) preserves reminders of the battle that put the Mississippi River into Union hands.

disrepair, and farms were overgrown or ruined. Blacks had been liberated but were landless and often homeless. Many whites faced poverty and homelessness as well. Mississippians had to start building a new world.

RECONSTRUCTION STRUGGLE

After the Civil War, the state was under the rule of a federal occupation force, but in 1868, Mississippians elected delegates to write a new state constitution. This was the first time black Mississippians were allowed to vote, and seventeen of the ninety-four elected delegates were black.

These delegates drew up the most democratic constitution in the state's history. The constitution extended the right to vote to all male citizens, including those who did not own property. Free public education was established for all children, black and white. Racial discrimination would no longer be legal. After one initial defeat, Mississippians voted to adopt this constitution. In 1870, federal occupation ended and Mississippi was readmitted to the Union.

Finally, blacks participated in the state and federal governments. In 1870, Hiram R. Revels, a Mississippian, became the first black to serve in the United States Senate. In the Mississippi state legislature, 36 of the 140 members were black. This era was a high point of political power for black Mississippians.

Many whites bitterly resented the fact that rights had been extended to blacks. Southern whites in particular blamed blacks for causing the Civil War, for the South's defeat in that war, and for the South's resulting poverty. These whites believed that blacks were an inferior race.

During the Reconstruction period, many white people worked to promote black involvement in state government. Two groups who were particularly influential were the scalawags and the carpetbaggers. Scalawags were white Mississippians who supported black civil rights in Mississippi. Carpetbaggers were white northerners who traveled to Mississippi and to other southern states to work for black civil rights. Although many of these people were sincere, some were driven only by thoughts of personal gain. Scalawags and carpetbaggers alike were detested by those whites who had no intention of accepting political or economic equality with former slaves.

Soon a new era of violence began. The Ku Klux Klan, an organization of masked terrorists, rose to enforce white supremacy. Blacks were often beaten and sometimes killed as a way of "keeping them in their place." Whites who were suspected of sympathizing with blacks were also terrorized.

Meridian, Mississippi, was the scene of grisly violence in 1871. Gunfire broke out in a courtroom, a judge was killed, and in the ensuing turmoil, thirty blacks were murdered. An investigation later showed that the blacks were unarmed and unable to defend themselves. The grim scene in Meridian foreshadowed the riots, violence, and lynchings that would scar Mississippi for the coming decades.

For a short time after the Civil War, Mississippi was a two-party state. Republicans and Democrats shared power. On a day-to-day level, blacks and whites shared transportation, restaurants, and other public facilities. Violence and fear changed all this. Civil rights were taken away from blacks. Strict segregation became not only the custom but the law in Mississippi, and racial politics would handicap the state for a long time to come.

The constitution of 1870 was unpopular with many whites. As

they gained political power, they wrote a new state constitution. The constitution of 1890 turned back the clock on civil rights. It prevented poor people, blacks in particular, from voting. Tax and residence requirements had to be met by voters. Furthermore, prospective voters could be asked to give a "reasonable interpretation" of any part of the state constitution. Because they were the sole judges of what might be a "reasonable interpretation," election officials now had the power to deny the vote at will.

The 1890 constitution was adopted without a vote by the people. Perhaps if it had been put to a popular vote, the constitution would have been rejected. As it stood, the constitution's effect was to freeze Mississippi politics and to guarantee that the people then in power would remain in power.

HOPE AND HARD TIMES

"What we had in my grandfather's day," said a Mississippian, "was mostly hope and hard times."

At the end of the nineteenth century, Mississippi lagged in prosperity, education, and civil rights. Despite its rich heritage in music and folklore and its considerable natural beauty, most people living in Mississippi had a hard and relentless struggle.

After the war, many of the great plantations were divided into smaller farms worked by tenant farmers. In the early 1900s, more than half of these tenant farmers were sharecroppers. In the sharecropping system, the landowner provided seed, fertilizer, tools, and work animals. The sharecroppers provided their own labor and the labor of their families. After a harvest, half—in some cases more—of the yield went to the landowner as a rent payment. The sharecroppers had to pay for all their needs out of

Tenant farming gradually disappeared between 1940 and 1970, and many tenant houses throughout rural Mississippi were abandoned.

their share of the harvest. There were other methods of tenant farming in Mississippi, but sharecropping was the most common.

Food for the sharecropper was often meager and housing was primitive. Bad weather, falling cotton prices, floods, and insect pests led to smaller harvests, but the landowner's share remained the same. Little by little, sharecropper families became indebted to the landowners. These debts tied the sharecroppers to the land they worked.

Usually, a sharecropper's children were needed to work in the fields. Sharecropper families had little chance of bettering themselves by hard work alone, and taking working children out of the fields to educate them was too costly. The system was discouraging; workers realized their efforts were often a losing battle. Yet Mississippians kept their courage and hope alive, believing that someday the state would offer prosperity and peace to all its residents.

Chapter 7

INTO THE TWENTIETH CENTURY

INTO THE TWENTIETH CENTURY

No educated man can be enslaved, for he knows
his rights and is willing to fight for them.
—Paul B. Johnson, Sr., governor of Mississippi, 1940-1943

Governor Paul B. Johnson, Sr., supported education with more than words. During Johnson's administration, textbooks were provided to all Mississippi students, whether black or white. Johnson sponsored help to the poor and elderly and maintained that women should be allowed to hold political offices.

Johnson was not typical of the leaders in Mississippi state politics during the early part of the twentieth century. More common were politicians who promoted racial hate to protect their own special interests. Eventually, such leaders would be replaced, but once again, change was slow in coming.

CAMPAIGNING IN THE PRIMARIES

A dramatic looking man standing on the front steps of a Mississippi courthouse speaks eloquently to a throng of citizens. His jet black hair, flowing from under a black hat, brushes his shoulders, while his pale skin and pure white suit offer striking contrast. From his lips pours a torrent of racial hate as he urges the closing of the already impoverished black schools. Blacks, he insists, must never be allowed to vote! He even praises lynching.

Such was the image presented by Mississippi politician and

master showman James K. Vardaman, governor from 1904 to 1908 and later a member of the United States Senate. Mississippi effectively had only one political party, the Democratic party.

Despite his fiery speeches, Vardaman did not close black schools once he was in office. Actually, he aided all schools and helped the state's numerous poor in several ways. The hatred he spouted when campaigning was designed to attract votes from whites who felt threatened by living in a state where blacks were a majority.

Vardaman resembled a number of politicians who rose through the primary system. Often elections were won or lost on personality rather than on issues.

The primaries, for all their stifling of democracy and their unfairness, produced some capable leaders. Among them was Hugh L. White, governor from 1936 to 1940, and again from 1952 to 1956. When White first took office, the country was in the midst of the worst depression in American history. Mississippi was particularly hard hit by the depression. White launched Balance Agriculture With Industry (BAWI), a program designed to attract factories to Mississippi. Mississippi did not industrialize overnight, but new low taxes and other inducements made manufacturing companies aware of Mississippi's potential. Slowly, some manufacturers accepted the invitation of BAWI, bringing new jobs to the state. BAWI was an important sign of awareness that Mississippi could not depend on farming forever, and it was a first step toward modernity.

WOMEN ENTER POLITICS

In 1890, the constitutional convention considered extending the vote to women, but it was not to be. Mississippi women, like women all over the country, began agitating for political rights.

Among Mississippi women who have been active in public life was Ida B. Wells. A co-founder of the National Association for the Advancement of Colored People (NAACP), Wells spent her life championing the rights of women and blacks.

Traditional education discouraged women from being active in business or politics, yet Mississippi women have long been active in public life. Eliza Jane Poitevent began her career in journalism as a poet and literary editor of the New Orleans *Times-Picayune*. She married the paper's publisher and inherited the paper at his death in 1876. At the age of twenty-seven, Poitevent found she owned a publication that was deeply in debt. Her shrewd policies saved the paper, and she became the first woman to own and publish an important daily newspaper in America.

Another example is Ida B. Wells. Wells was born in 1864 of parents who had been slaves, and she was orphaned at a young age. She paid her own way through college, raised her younger brothers and sisters, and then taught in rural schools. Her bold protests against injustices to blacks caused her to be forced out of teaching. She became a writer, editor, and lecturer. All her life she struggled for the rights of women and blacks.

Women gained the right to vote in 1920, and two years later Belle Kearney ran for the United States Senate. She failed in this attempt. Undiscouraged, Kearney kept working in politics and in

After World War II, black southerners, especially those who had served in the armed forces, were increasingly dissatisfied with the injustices of segregation.

1924 won a seat in the Mississippi State Senate, becoming the first woman in the South to gain such a position.

World War II brought many changes in the feelings of women. Some women who worked in factories and did "men's jobs" during the war decided they could do men's jobs in politics, too. Women had begun to see that they could play an important role in shaping the future. It was 1968 before women gained the right to sit on Mississippi juries. Yet women continued working for their rights.

During the time that women were gradually gaining rights, blacks throughout the South were becoming increasingly dissatisfied and restless. Widespread service in the United States armed forces had given black Mississippians a broader view of the world and a greater sense of their own ability, dignity, and worth. Their sense of injustice would soon erupt into sharp conflict and force a great advancement in Mississippi.

CIVIL RIGHTS CONFLICT: OLD WAYS CHALLENGED

In the middle of the twentieth century, the racial scene throughout the Deep South, including Mississippi, was marked by glaring and long-standing inequality. The South claimed to offer separate, but equal, education under segregation, but black schools were consistently shortchanged. Blacks were barred from restaurants patronized by whites and were excluded from public swimming pools, public parks, and most libraries. Public transportation was strictly segregated. White primaries had been declared illegal by the United States Supreme Court a decade before, yet fear and terrorism kept black voters away from the polls.

Then in 1954, the United States Supreme Court determined that racial segregation in schools was unlawful. Whites in all the southern states felt as though a Gulf hurricane had swept across the land. Threats and counterthreats rang throughout the South. Mississippi's governor, Hugh L. White, tried to pursue a moderate policy but announced that the state would "legally resist." But the era of compromise and surrender on civil rights for blacks was over. Black groups all over Mississippi demanded that the court decision be respected, now. At the same time, whites formed citizens' councils to preserve the old ways.

The citizens' councils quickly gained power and soon exerted heavy, if indirect, pressure. For instance, many black people who signed petitions for integration of the schools lost their jobs and found their credit cut off at stores. Taunts and jeers forced civil-rights activists to leave their home communities. Newspapers that took a moderate stand lost advertisers and subscribers, yet several courageous white Mississippi editors opposed the councils—and paid a high price.

Civil-rights protests during the 1960s (right) and the admission of James Meredith (above) to Ole Miss angered Mississippi whites.

Blacks actively challenged laws upholding segregation on every front; white resistance hardened. There were murders and lynchings. At the end of the 1950s, it seemed that real equality for black Mississippians had hardly inched forward.

In 1962, James Meredith, a black air-force veteran, won a legal battle to uphold his right to enroll at the University of Mississippi. The admission of a black student to "Ole Miss" enraged the segregationists. Governor Ross Barnett challenged the federal government and urged Mississippians to resist.

A street disturbance begun by Ole Miss students expanded alarmingly as armed nonstudents and other outsiders arrived in force. In 1962, Meredith, accompanied by federal marshals, arrived for classes. The federal marshals and twenty thousand troops quelled a riot that erupted in Oxford, home of the university. Despite the violence, Meredith became a student at Ole Miss, a turning point but by no means the end of the struggle.

In the summer of 1964, about a thousand volunteers, black and white, of all ages and from many states, came to Mississippi to support desegregation and black political rights. Mississippi whites retaliated with violence. Three of the volunteers were murdered and thirty-seven black churches were burned.

In the summer of 1964, volunteers from all over the country came to Mississippi to support desegregation and black political rights.

Lawlessness cost Mississippi dearly. Strife continued into 1967, even though many white Mississippians were disgusted and ashamed of the bombings and shootings. The image of the state was tarnished, and industrialists did not want to build new plants in troubled areas.

Yet even during the time of violence, cracks were appearing in the walls of segregation. Mississippi State University traditionally refused to play against any racially integrated team. In 1963, the school's outstanding basketball team won the Southeastern Conference. That year the team went on to play in higher national competition, breaking the color-line tradition. Within a few years, high-school athletic teams dropped their color-line requirements.

Cultural pastimes did not escape from the pressure of integration. Many famous singers, orchestras, and actors refused to perform for segregated or white-only audiences. Theaters, concert halls, and hotels that insisted on separate arrangements for black entertainers were pressured as well. They had a choice: change policy or lose the best artists—and revenue. Because of these pressures, Leontyne Price, a great soprano, sang for an integrated audience in her hometown of Laurel, Mississippi. The event was especially heartening because Leontyne Price was black.

The national Voting Rights Act of 1965 resulted in the registering of about 130,000 new black voters in Mississippi, a sure sign that the old political order could not last. In 1967, John Bell Williams, a segregationist, was elected governor. Yet the election was remarkable because twenty-two blacks were also elected to state offices. This was the start of a new era in Mississippi. Robert Clark, one of the blacks elected, was still serving in the Mississippi house of representatives more than twenty years later.

After the hardest years of the civil-rights struggle, many Mississippians claimed proudly that racial harmony in the state began to move forward faster than in other states. Blacks and whites, they said, had always been neighbors in Mississippi, so once the gates were open, progress came swiftly.

THE NEW FARMS

For generations, farm-family income in Mississippi has often been the lowest or nearly the lowest in the nation. Among the factors that worked to keep farm income low were worn-out soil, boll weevils, low cotton prices, floods, and depressions. Mississippi has attacked these problems, solving some and lessening others.

In the days when cotton ruled the state, there was no indication that Mississippi would have to learn to rely on other sources of income. But cotton quickly wore out the land. In the rich Delta and Black Prairie regions it could be grown year after year, but the thinner soil of other parts of Mississippi could not support continued planting of the crop.

When cotton prices fell, Mississippi suffered, for there was little else to fall back on. Heavy concentration on a single crop

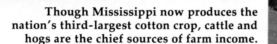

Though Mississippi now produces the
nation's third-largest cotton crop, cattle and
hogs are the chief sources of farm income.

caused Mississippians to neglect other types of agriculture and
industry.

In 1907, a cotton-destroying insect, the boll weevil, invaded
Mississippi from the Southwest. The pest caused great hardship.
Countless Mississippi farmers lost everything because of the
insect, providing proof that it was risky to depend heavily on a
single crop. Modern chemicals and methods of farming have made
it possible to control insect attacks and to minimize cotton's
depletion of the soil. Yet there are parts of Mississippi that never
returned to relying on cotton after the boll-weevil plague.

Dethroning King Cotton was a major stride forward.
Mississippi now produces the nation's third-largest cotton crop,
but cotton is only part of the produce of Mississippi's farms. Cattle

Since Mississippi Delta farmers have converted older cotton fields to catfish ponds (right and above), the state has become the world's number one producer of grain-fed catfish.

and hogs are the chief sources of farm income. Rice, corn, wheat, soybeans, and poultry have gained in importance as cash crops. Mississippi Delta farmers recently converted older cotton fields to catfish ponds. The new farms have greatly increased the economic base in this region of the state, and Mississippi is now the world's number-one producer of grain-fed catfish.

Machinery radically changed life on most farms. Tractors replaced draft animals, and incubators and milking machines came into use. A mechanical cotton picker is twenty times as efficient as a human worker harvesting a crop. The mechanical picker and the use of chemicals for "chopping cotton" have contributed to the end of widespread sharecropping.

Efficient farming requires much equipment, however, and the large investment is often beyond the means of the typical

Rice has become an
important cash crop
for Mississippi.
Left: Rice harvesting
Above: A rice mill

Mississippi landowner. So although farm income has risen
steadily in the past few years, fewer farmers can earn a living
from their own small fields or from those they rent. Most of the
gain now goes to the large farms that can afford modern methods,
making the future of large-scale farming in Mississippi very
promising.

The change from small farms has not necessarily meant the end
of small-town life. Instead, more efficient and diversified farming
has attracted many food-related industries. Plants engaged in food
processing, canning, frozen packing, and the treatment of poultry
products are best placed near the source of the products. Thus,
such plants have been established in the rural areas of the state,
contributing to the attractiveness of small-town life.

Pascagoula, whose history in the field of shipbuilding goes back to the Ingalls Corporation's contributions to the World War II effort, now leases this modern shipyard to Litton Industries. Ingalls is now part of the Litton operation.

THE GROWTH OF INDUSTRY

Today, manufacturing creates one-fourth of Mississippi's gross state product and employs one-fourth of all the state's workers. Not only does the state employ more manufacturing workers than ever before, but these workers outnumber farm workers by more than three to one. This is an astonishing change for a state that was predominantly agricultural only four decades ago.

A good deal of this success began with the Balance Agriculture With Industry program. An example is the Ingalls Shipbuilding Corporation at Pascagoula. The huge Ingalls yards built all-welded ships during World War II, making an important contribution to the nation's defense effort. After the war, the company expanded into making luxury liners, atomic submarines, and various types of cargo vessels.

The launching of a new ship is always an exciting event.

The Research and Development Center in Jackson is a state agency devoted to helping the expansion of industry and bringing new manufacturing enterprises to the state. One of the agency's successes is the modern shipyard at Pascagoula. This state-financed endeavor was leased to Litton Ship Systems and has created jobs for a growing industrial work force. Ingalls is now part of Litton Industries.

In 1965, Peavey Electronics was established in Meridian. The company is now the world's largest producer of electronic musical instruments and has plants in Decatur and Morton. Insurance companies and health care centers have expanded. Baxter-Travenol Laboratories is a new employer in the town of Cleveland.

Twenty years ago, a Biloxi businessman complained about the state's slow progress. "Mississippi can't travel through the space age in a mule cart," he said.

His worry proved unfounded. Mississippi entered the Space Age as well as the computer era with new industries, new jobs, and new confidence in the future.

Chapter 8

GOVERNMENT AND THE ECONOMY

GOVERNMENT AND THE ECONOMY

In 1987, Mississippi voters elected Ray Mabus, Jr., governor. At thirty-nine, Mabus became one of the youngest governors in the nation. On learning of his election victory, he announced, "Change has come. Mississippi will never be last again!" He had campaigned for office denouncing "old-time politics and the old-time politicians." He demanded better schools and declared he would aggressively seek new industries for the state.

His opponent in the contest, Jack Reed, had supported many of the same things. Reed drew 47 percent of the vote and lost the race. Yet Reed had garnered a larger percentage of votes than had any Republican candidate running for a state office in more than a century.

This was a race between two progressive candidates, and it was clear that no matter which became governor, the winner would be Mississippi. The state was determined once again to move ahead, leaving behind some of its troubled past.

GOVERNMENT

The state government of Mississippi is similar to the federal government in Washington, D.C. The legislative branch is responsible for making laws and allocating money; the judicial branch interprets the laws; the executive branch, headed by the governor, is responsible for administering the state's laws and business.

The legislature is divided into a senate of 52 members and a house of representatives of 122 members. They meet in the state capitol in Jackson to suggest, debate, and enact laws.

The governor is elected for a four-year term, and since a 1986 amendment to the constitution may now serve two consecutive terms. Most of the important executive officers are elected directly by the voters. These officers include the lieutenant governor, secretary of state, attorney general, auditor, and treasurer.

The highest court in the state's judicial system is the supreme court, made up of nine elected judges. Chancery courts handle civil cases and circuit courts hear both civil and criminal matters. County and juvenile courts also administer justice.

Mississippi's eighty-two counties are each administered by five elected supervisors from different districts. County government is important in Mississippi. Traditionally, county courthouses have been gathering places as well as centers of law and politics. Most cities are governed by a mayor and council.

About 70 percent of the government's income comes from taxes. A sales tax on purchased goods is the largest single source of revenue. About 30 percent of the government's income comes from federal grants and programs.

EDUCATION

"The safety of a government is best ensured by the education of its people." Governor Albert Gallatin Brown offered this premise in 1846, as he tried to establish a statewide free public school system in Mississippi. His hope had very little success—a statewide school system was not established until 1869.

Uniform textbooks began to be supplied to all students in 1904. Rural schools were started in 1906, and the first agricultural high

The University of Southern Mississippi (left) and the Mississippi University for Women (above), are among the state's sixteen accredited universities and colleges.

schools in the state were founded in 1908. Vocational and technical schools were established after World War II to meet the demands of new industry in the state. In the early 1940s, Governor Paul B. Johnson, Sr., made certain that books were free to all students, whether black or white.

Now, all public school districts are integrated. School attendance is required for children six through thirteen years old.

Jefferson College, in Washington, began its first classes in 1811, six years before Mississippi was admitted to the Union. Elizabeth Female Academy was founded in the same town in 1818 and was one of the first institutions in America to grant degrees to women. Today, sixteen Mississippi colleges and universities are fully accredited by the Southern Association of Colleges and Schools. The state's teaching medical school is located at Jackson. The University of Mississippi Medical Center has received international attention for its medical research and numerous transplant operations.

The Old Capitol, in Jackson, houses the State Historical Museum.

Museums and libraries are also important to education in Mississippi. One of the nation's best collections of historical documents is housed in the Charlotte Capers Building in Jackson and is available to scholars and researchers. Visitors can see exhibits focusing on history in the Old Capitol, also in Jackson. In Vicksburg, the collection of Confederate memorabilia in the Old Court House Museum is of unusual interest. The Mississippi Museum of Natural Sciences in Jackson displays exhibits dramatizing and illustrating natural history. Libraries are scattered throughout the state; more than 250 of them are open to the public. Several colleges and universities also have excellent libraries.

Mississippi schools still find that tax money is in short supply. Although the average dollar spent per pupil is relatively low, the percentage of personal income devoted to education is higher in Mississippi than in many other states. Improvement of all levels of education in Mississippi is an announced goal of the state's political leaders.

The expansion of Mississippi's sawmills has created several new industries in the state, including furniture making.

INDUSTRY

Strides made by the Balance Agriculture With Industry program are in evidence today. Because the majority of Mississippians are employed in manufacturing activities, the state is no longer dependent solely on agriculture. For the last few decades, more people were employed in the manufacture of clothing than in other manufacturing activities.

The modern shipbuilding facility leased to Litton Industries has made shipbuilding the mainstay of Pascagoula. The manufacture of transportation-related products, shipbuilding in particular, is now the state's number one source of employment.

Electrical equipment and machinery production is flourishing as factories turn out complex switchboards and transformers as well as familiar household appliances.

Careful control and reforestation programs have brought back Mississippi's lumber industry.

Chemicals for use in the state's agriculture and for export are important Mississippi products now, as are plastics and synthetics.

Before 1950, lumbering was a major source of income. However, most of the state's virgin forests were cut down by 1920, and much of that lumbering was done by out-of-state corporations. Today, careful control and reforestation programs have brought back the lumbering industry. Sawmills have expanded and new industries have resulted—factories now make plywood, mobile homes, boxes, containers, and furniture. Large plants producing wood products flourish in Vicksburg, Philadelphia, Laurel, Greenville, and Tupelo.

Service industries—activities such as trade, finance, and community service—account for almost two-thirds of the gross state product and employ more than half of the state's work force.

Commercial fishermen in Mississippi bring in
catches that include shrimp (above), oysters
(right), and a variety of saltwater fish
(top right) such as menhaden and red snapper.

Nearly 165,000 Mississippians are employed in wholesale and
retail selling, and 180,000 work for the government, including
many who are employed at Mississippi military bases. Personal,
social, and community services create about 125,000 jobs.

Each year, about 25 million barrels of petroleum are pumped
from more than 4,000 oil wells in Mississippi. The state is also a
rich producer of natural gas.

Some of the most delicious shrimp, oysters, and red snapper
that appear on American dining tables are brought from
Mississippi waters. Biloxi has become a large center for shrimp
packing and Pascagoula is important in commercial fishing. The
annual catch returns about $50 million.

Mississippi livestock farmers raise hogs (above) and sheep as well as cattle. Soybeans (right) are the state's second most important crop, after cotton.

AGRICULTURE

Approximately half the area of Mississippi remains agricultural land and is divided into about 39,000 farms. Cotton, though no longer as dominant as in former times, yields about one-fourth of farm income. Soybeans are second in value, and rice and sweet potatoes are also important agricultural products. Various grains thrive in the state as do pecans and peanuts.

The poultry industry, enhanced by modern methods, has expanded. Mississippi ranks high in the nation in the production of "broilers," chickens from eight to twelve weeks old. Hogs and sheep account for a portion of farm income, and even more important are beef and dairy cattle. Fruits and vegetables from the state's truck farms are ample and varied.

TRANSPORTATION AND COMMUNICATION

Mississippi is proud of its modern highway system, which includes 10,900 miles (17,542 kilometers) of surfaced highways and a network of nonsurfaced roads.

The state is dotted with airports, and three scheduled airlines offer national and international service. Fifteen railroads on 3,500 miles (5,633 kilometers) of track provide transportation for freight, and more than a dozen cities enjoy rail passenger service.

Mississippi owes its earliest development to river transportation, and the Mississippi River is still important to the nation's—as well as the state's—commerce. Natchez, Greenville, and Vicksburg are major river ports, and the Tennessee-Tombigbee Waterway gives towns in northeast Mississippi access to the Gulf.

Twenty-two daily newspapers are published in the state, along with numerous weeklies and periodicals. The tradition of journalism dates back to 1799 when the state's first paper, the *Mississippi Gazette*, was founded in Natchez. Today, the largest dailies in circulation are the *Daily Herald/The Sun* in Biloxi, the *Jackson Daily News*, the Jackson *Clarion-Ledger*, and the *Northeast Mississippi Daily Journal*, of Tupelo.

Mississippi has 18 television stations and 179 radio broadcasting stations. For many years, radio was the only link between many Mississippi farms and the broader world. Now, both radio and television reach every corner of the state.

Chapter 9

ARTS AND LEISURE

ARTS AND LEISURE

Over the generations, Mississipians have known their share of war, poverty, toil, and struggle. They survived these hardships with an endurance sustained by hope. It is not surprising that endurance and hope are powerful themes in Mississippi's music and literature. The songs and the writings of Mississippi people are among the state's greatest, most abundant treasures.

MUSIC: FOLK SONGS TO SYMPHONIES

The native music of Mississippi has deep roots in the lives of the people. Religion has played an important role in the daily life of many Mississippians. The singing of hymns adds pleasure and joy to Mississippi church services. Country people sometimes gather to spend a day singing religious songs.

No American music is more beautiful and inspiring than the black religious songs known as spirituals. One of the most moving of these reveals the confusion and insecurity of the slaves: "Sometimes I Feel Like a Motherless Child." Gospel music, still popular today, developed a little later than the traditional spiritual, but it, too, speaks of hardship and hope. Both blacks and whites adopted gospel music.

Slaves brought with them the African tradition of group singing while at work. The chants and rhythmical shouts that developed from this are known as work songs. Workers on levees and railroad tracks thus made their own special music.

One of the most famous Mississippi songs—and legends—is the story of Casey Jones, a railroad engineer. In 1900, Jones left Memphis, Tennessee, driving his engine on a lightning run across Mississippi toward the town of Canton. On seeing a train stalled on the track ahead, Jones deliberately derailed his own engine to save the lives of others. Today, all Americans sing of his courage in meeting death at Vaughn, Mississippi.

Another Mississippi song with an unusual story is "The Midnight Special." Prisoners at Parchman State Farm looked forward to the arrival of a special train. Two or three times a year, the train left Jackson at midnight to bring visitors to the prison. Convicts often were working in the fields before dawn, and if the train's headlight shone on a man he would—according to legend—be the next one freed. Thus came the inspiration for the words to the song "Let the Midnight Special shine her light on me . . . "

Delta Blues, music that grew up among sharecroppers in the Mississippi Delta, is a great contribution to American music. Black singers, taking their music with them, moved north and the blues flourished, especially in Chicago. Big Bill Broonzy, Robert Johnson, and Mississippi John Hurt were among the best of these musicians. B. B. King, Muddy Waters, Bo Diddley, and other Mississippians helped spread Delta Blues throughout the world.

White Mississippians developed a style of their own now known as country music. Jimmie Rodgers of Meridian was the first star to be recognized by the Country Music Hall of Fame. Elvis Presley, born in Tupelo, began as a singer of country music often touched with gospel, but won stardom with rock-and-roll performances.

Noted opera soprano Leontyne Price (left), rock-and-roll star Elvis Presley (top), and Delta Blues musicians Muddy Waters (above) and B.B. King (right) are among the Mississippians who have made lasting contributions to the music world.

Leontyne Price, the great soprano, is Mississippi's most-celebrated figure in the world of classical music. When the New York Metropolitan Opera opened at its new home in Lincoln Center, Leontyne Price starred that gala night as the leading soprano. Her career on the opera and concert stages has been brilliant. Meridian has given the world of opera two other outstanding singers in John Anderson and Gail Robinson.

Five symphony orchestras have been established in Mississippi cities. The oldest, in Jackson, began performing in 1943. College groups also play classical music and both universities and community associations support visiting musicians.

The Mississippi Opera Association has pioneered in presenting opera to state audiences, while universities from time to time offer opera workshops and sometimes full-scale productions.

Composer William Grant Still has created symphonies and shorter works of classical music, often in the Afro-American tradition, and Milton Babbit has been praised for contemporary works, including his *Composition for Synthesizer*.

LITERATURE

Book-loving Mississippians like to claim that their state has produced more writers per capita than any other. Whether or not that statement is true, there is no doubt that Mississippi writers are a large and impressive group.

William Faulkner, who received the 1949 Nobel Prize for literature, brought northern Mississippi to life on paper. His masterpieces, such as *Light in August*, rank high in world literature. His stories showed his state to the world, as he wrote of all types of Mississippians—of Indians, of blacks, and of whites.

Eudora Welty, Mississippi's great woman of letters, drew on life in her home state to recreate the past and present of Mississippi in remarkable novels and short stories. With a sharp but loving eye and a keen ear, she has revealed the daily life and talk of small towns as well as the intense drama beneath their surfaces. Welty received the 1973 Pulitzer Prize in fiction for *The Optimist's Daughter*.

Richard Wright had a rare grasp of the lives and feelings of his fellow black Americans. He vividly pictured his own Mississippi childhood in *Black Boy*, an autobiography.

Excellence in newspaper editorial writing seems part of Mississippi's literary tradition. Hodding Carter, Hazel Brannon

Probably the greatest of Mississippi's many distinguished writers was William Faulkner (far right). Eudora Welty (top) wrote memorable novels and short stories. Many of the powerful dramas written by Tennessee Williams (right) were set in Mississippi.

Smith, and Ira Harkey are Mississippians who have received the Pulitzer Prize in journalism for their distinguished editorials.

Mississippi's gift to the theater was Tennessee Williams of Columbus. Williams, a two-time winner of the Pulitzer Prize in drama, caught the rhythms and music of southern speech and fashioned everyday talk into dialogue of poetic beauty. Small Mississippi towns were often the background for his powerful dramas. Williams' best-known play is *A Streetcar Named Desire*.

ART

Mississippi has produced a number of outstanding painters and sculptors. Oxford painter Theora Hamblett creates charming but strong Mississippi scenes in a primitive style. Marie Hull is a talented painter working in Jackson. Another rising young artist is Glannray Tutor from Oxford. Richard Barthe is ranked as one of the country's best sculptors.

The Mississippi Art Workshop has encouraged art in the state. Nearly all Mississippi colleges not only have art departments for instruction but also galleries to show the work of students, teachers, and visiting artists.

PERFORMING ARTS

Mississippi has enjoyed a lively tradition of stage performances. Showboats brought plays and musical entertainment to the river ports. Other touring troupes, some traveling by river and others by rail, appeared in the larger cities, especially Jackson.

The Jackson Little Theater, now called New Stage, began presenting plays in 1925, which makes it one of the oldest continuously operating theater groups in the United States. Today, at least twenty-one other theater companies perform in the state.

New York theater has drawn on Mississippi talent. Lehman Engel was a Broadway director and conductor of musicals. Playwright Mart Crowley wrote the successful *The Boys in the Band*. One of the finest American stage actors is James Earl Jones. Stella Stevens, Mary Ann Mobley, and Dana Andrews are among many Mississippians who have appeared prominently in films and television.

Every year, all the arts of the state meet at a week-long Mississippi Arts Festival in Jackson. It is a fascinating medley of folk music, jazz, blues, and rock. Audiences can listen to choral singing and the Jackson Symphony Orchestra, and can see plays, dances, marching bands, puppets, and art exhibits. This is a dazzling week for the audiences and a proud week for Mississippi.

Colorful Choctaw dances and exciting stickball games are part of the festivities at the Choctaw Indian Fair.

A different kind of event is the Choctaw Indian Fair in July. It is held in Philadelphia, a town built on Choctaw Indian land. Several thousand Choctaws still make their homes in this area. Along with other attractions, Choctaw crafts and products are displayed at this midsummer fair.

FAIRS, FIDDLERS, AND PILGRIMAGES

The Mississippi State Fair sparkles in Jackson every October. Here is agriculture and industry on parade, with scores of exhibits ranging from cows to computers, milking machines to marmalades. The fair displays a cross-section of the state's agriculture, industry, and commerce. For many farmers, livestock breeders, and even handcraft artisans, winning a ribbon in competition at the fair is the ultimate thrill. Tens of thousands of people stroll along a brilliantly lighted midway, enjoy the games and shows of a giant carnival, listen to musical stars, and compete in various contests.

Big, well-attended county fairs are enjoyed all over the state. The Neshoba County Fair, held every August near Philadelphia, is

The International Ballet Competition in Jackson (above) draws competitors from all over the world.

Young fairgoers enjoy a carnival ride at the Mississippi State Fair (left).

the biggest and best known. The fair lasts seven days and is highlighted by harness racing, a midway, and concerts. The fair attracts nationwide attention because of the number of presidential candidates who attend and give speeches.

Wherever a visitor travels in the state, a horse show is probably only a short gallop away. The Mississippi State Horse Show in Jackson is a remarkable demonstration of horses trotting, walking, and jumping.

Many tuneful, foot-tapping celebrations are held in Mississippi annually. One of the outstanding ones is the Jimmie Rodgers Memorial Festival in the celebrated songwriter's hometown of Meridian. Country-and-western music fills the air as country stars and stars-to-be perform before cheering audiences. The Delta Blues Festival in Greenville is dedicated to music that goes back to the sharecroppers of the Delta.

Jackson is the site of the International Ballet Competition. This event, held every four years, attracts competitors from all over the world.

The annual Delta Blues Festival in Greenville attracts huge crowds.

At Pascagoula, Pass Christian, and Biloxi, the citizens turn out for Mardi Gras celebrations, carnivals, parades, and masked balls held on Shrove Tuesday, the day before Lent begins.

Many Mississippians would insist that the best state celebration is the Blessing of the Fleet, more commonly called the Biloxi Shrimp Festival. The custom of blessing a fleet is a very old tradition going back to Europe. During the first week in June, dancing takes place in the streets, boats with special decorations parade on the water, and the shrimp fleet is blessed for the coming season. Hundreds of vessels participate in this festival; their crews are mostly descendants of French and Yugoslavian settlers.

"Pilgrimages" in Mississippi are tours of historic mansions and gardens that give a glimpse of the home life of wealthy Mississippians during the antebellum era. The guides are

Guides dressed in period costumes conduct tours of historic mansions during the annual pilgrimage in Columbus (above).
One of the most famous—and most colorful—state festivals is the Blessing of the Fleet (left), when the specially decorated shrimp boats are blessed for the coming season.

costumed in lovely hoop skirts in the style of the period in which the mansions were built. Some of the pilgrimages are annual events, others are held nearly year-round. The most famous pilgrimage takes place in Natchez, where it is combined with a Confederate pageant. The Gulf Coast cities also display their stately homes and lovely gardens. Cities such as Columbus, Port Gibson, Holly Springs, Macon, Oxford, Yazoo City, Aberdeen, and Vicksburg offer inviting pilgrimages.

SPORTS

As in most states, football, baseball, and basketball dominate the field of competitive athletics, although in recent years Mississippi has produced some very good tennis players.

At least three members of this Mississippi State baseball team went on to play in the major leagues: Will Clark, Rafael Palmeiro, and Bobby Thigpen.

Baseball was the first sport to gain wide popularity in the small towns of Mississippi, and even the poorest community could field some sort of baseball team, even in hard times. Sometimes traveling "professional" teams came through in battered cars or buses to take on local favorites.

Today, baseball is played in all parts of the state from Little League through high school and college programs. Will Clark of Mississippi State sparked the United States team during the 1984 Olympic exhibition games at Los Angeles. He continued to win fame in professional sports with the San Francisco Giants and Texas Rangers and is one of America's outstanding athletes.

In football, Mississippi's "Big Three" are the Mississippi State Bulldogs, the Golden Eagles of the University of Southern Mississippi at Hattiesburg, and the University of Mississippi (Ole Miss), which fields the famed Rebels. Over the years, the Rebels and then the Eagles have been a major force in national competition. Walter Payton played college football at Jackson State

Crab netters try their luck in the waters off Gulfport.

University and went on to become the National Football League's leading rusher. He retired from the Chicago Bears at the end of the 1987-88 season.

Basketball is popular throughout the state, and each year some fine high-school and college teams bring cheering fans to their feet.

Mississippi has a number of challenging golf courses, with some of the best ones at Jackson, Greenville, Hattiesburg, and in the Gulfport-Biloxi area.

The creation of large artificial lakes such as the Ross R. Barnett Reservoir prompted an upsurge in water sports. These lakes have modern facilities for waterskiing, swimming, and boating.

Gulfport has an excellent small-craft harbor, site of the annual Mississippi Deep Sea Fishing Rodeo, where fishermen from all over the United States, Canada, and Latin America compete in various types of sport fishing every July.

Game is plentiful in the forests of Mississippi, and the state has many quiet streams and lakes for fishing.

Chapter 10

HIGHLIGHTS OF THE MAGNOLIA STATE

HIGHLIGHTS OF THE MAGNOLIA STATE

Mississippi comfortably blends its many contrasts: quaint old courthouse towns mix easily with modern highways; luxury hotels on sandy beaches complement rustic country inns; the quiet of the pine forest balances the rushing rivers of spring. The Gulf Coast resorts are well-known havens for countless winter visitors. Less famous, but equally inviting, are the state's six national forests and the mellow river ports with their pillared mansions. A quick tour from Mississippi's northern hills to the coastal waters offers beauty, history, and charm.

NORTHERN MISSISSIPPI

The magnificent Natchez Trace Parkway enters Mississippi in the extreme northeast corner of the state, a region of high hills and rolling forests. The complete parkway is a broad, 444-mile (715-kilometer) highway that crosses and recrosses the original Natchez Trace of historic fame. At parkway headquarters, north of Tupelo, is a museum that brings to life the story of the Trace and its early travelers. Along the parkway, inviting, scenic trails are clearly marked, and wayside exhibits and craft demonstrations provide entertainment and education.

Tupelo is the northernmost city along the parkway. Just outside the town stands Chickasaw Village, which marks the approximate location of a fortified Chickasaw Indian town. In Tupelo itself, the

A scenic trail along the
Natchez Trace Parkway

house where Elvis Presley was born is now open to the public as a small museum.

Tupelo National Battlefield was the site of a Civil War struggle. The Confederate troops there were led by colorful Mississippi cavalryman General Nathan Bedford Forrest. The battle at Tupelo was fierce and terrible. A Confederate observer commented that Forrest's army, under the command of Stephen D. Lee, was "sent in piecemeal—and slaughtered wholesale." Today, the battlefield is a park near the spot where the Confederate attack was launched against the Union position.

Also at Tupelo is the National Fish Hatchery, which maintains fifteen huge ponds. This warm-water hatchery produces bluegills, large-mouth bass, red-ear sunfish, and channel catfish for distribution. Every year, three million fish are sent to farm ponds and reservoirs in thirty-eight northern Mississippi counties.

Just south of Tupelo, Tombigbee State Park attracts visitors who enjoy boating, fishing, swimming, and waterskiing.

Southeast of Tupelo, on the Tombigbee River, stands the town of Columbus. In 1817, General Andrew Jackson ordered a military road built between New Orleans and Nashville. Columbus grew up along that road. More than a hundred antebellum homes beautify Columbus. A short distance from town is the especially fine Waverly Plantation. Its twin circular staircases rise to an observation cupola offering a panoramic view.

Columbus thrived and could support such mansions because it was at the center of the soil-rich "Black Prairie." The state's first public school opened here in 1821. The town was also the site of the first state-supported women-only school in the United States.

Southwest of Columbus, the Tombigbee National Forest spreads over 62,500 acres (25,293 hectares) of beautiful land complete with two large lakes.

Greenwood, a city of about twenty-five thousand people, is one of the nation's largest and busiest cotton markets. Located on the Yazoo River, it early became a flourishing inland port. Rich, black Delta land stretches around Greenwood.

The nearby Florewood River Plantation, a state park and museum, allows visitors to see life as it was on a plantation in the 1850s. Crops are worked and harvested in the old manner, and craft demonstrations are offered. The plantation has twenty-two restored buildings.

Greenville, one of the state's largest Mississippi River ports, uses a protected lake for a harbor. Some of the mighty levees that hold back the unruly river have been built here. Marine building and repair companies are the backbone of Greenville's economy, and the city is home to a large fleet of boats and barges. North of Greenville lies Winterville Mounds State Historic Site, marking an area that was once the center of an ancient Indian culture. A high central mound and fourteen smaller mounds may have been shrines for worship of the sun.

Oxford is the home of the University of Mississippi. The wooded, hilly campus is a major cultural center. In addition to the

Liberty Hall (top) is among the more than one hundred antebellum, or pre-Civil War, homes in Columbus. Many of these homes are surrounded by formal gardens (above).
William Faulkner owned Rowan Oak (middle right), an antebellum home in Oxford that is now a Faulkner museum.
Florewood River Plantation near Greenwood (right) is a state park and living-history museum.

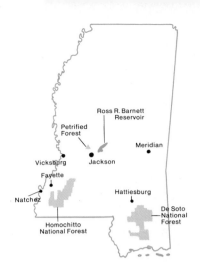

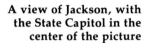

A view of Jackson, with the State Capitol in the center of the picture

attractive buildings devoted to classes and housing, there are three museums and an art gallery on the campus. Rowan Oak in Oxford, the home of writer William Faulkner, is now maintained as a museum by the university. Each August, the university conducts a Faulkner conference that attracts scholars from Russia, China, and Japan as well as many European countries.

SOUTHERN MISSISSIPPI

Jackson, the state capital and largest city, is impressively situated on the bluffs of the Pearl River. The center of the city is laid out in a checkerboard pattern suggested by Thomas Jefferson. Jackson is very much the heart and hub of Mississippi, the center not only of government but of commerce and manufacturing, a junction point of highways and railroads.

The State Capitol rises tall and imposing, a structure symbolizing authority. The nearby governor's mansion, built in 1842, covers an entire city block. The State Historical Museum,

The Mississippi Petrified Forest, near Flora, contains giant prehistoric logs that have turned to stone.

one of the finest of its kind in the United States, occupies the building that was once the state capitol. The history of the state is graphically shown in the museum's exhibits. The crucial secession convention of 1861 was held inside these walls.

When Jackson was besieged by Union troops in 1863, General William Tecumseh Sherman stayed in The Oaks, a cottage of hand-hewn timber that is now open to the public.

Probably the most enchanting spot in Jackson is lovely Mynelle Gardens, a bird sanctuary ablaze with flowers and blossoming shrubs. Here are blooming gardens of wildflowers and tropical plants as well as a Japanese garden.

Natural history is dramatically presented at the Museum of Natural Science in Jackson. The research collection has fifty thousand specimens. Equally interesting is the Jackson Zoological Park, which houses four hundred mammals, birds, and reptiles in simulated natural environments.

North of Jackson, at Flora, is the Mississippi Petrified Forest, a fascinating place where a prehistoric river deposited giant logs as

The Illinois Memorial at Vicksburg National Military Park

driftwood. There is a nature trail and a museum with natural history exhibits.

The Ross R. Barnett Reservoir, northeast of Jackson on the Natchez Trace Parkway, is a large artificial lake that is a major recreational attraction in the Jackson area.

The river town of Vicksburg is almost surrounded by a national military park. The park gives visitors a dramatic reminder of the Civil War and of the people who lived through it. Still evident are the tunnels, trenches, and caves dug by citizens trying to escape the ferocious shelling. The largest collection of Civil War relics in the world is housed in the Old Court House Museum.

Vicksburg has restored and furnished many historic antebellum houses, including Planters Hall, McRaven, and Cedar Grove. The Army Corps of Engineers conducts guided tours of its fascinating Waterways Experiment Station.

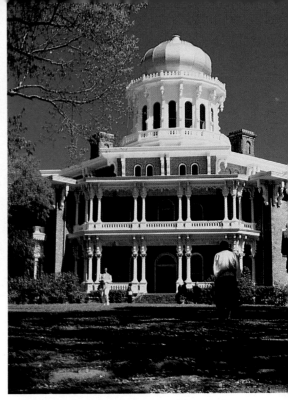

Stanton Hall (above) and Longwood (right) are two of the antebellum houses in Natchez that are included in the Natchez Pilgrimage tours.

Natchez, at the southern end of the Natchez Trace Parkway, is one of America's most charming and picturesque towns. Yet Natchez has factories and prosperous commerce. The old town was founded in 1716 for practical business reasons—as a center for trade in furs and bear grease. But now it is a living museum. Spanish, French, British, Confederate, and United States flags have fluttered over Natchez in the course of its eventful history.

Connelly's Tavern, built around 1795 on a hillside overlooking the Mississippi River, was once the last outpost of civilization on the southwest frontier of America, the jumping-off place for the wilderness beyond. Even older is King's Tavern in Natchez, which began serving the public in 1789.

Stanton Hall is a handsome mansion set in a cluster of giant live oaks. Just before the Civil War, construction was started on Longwood, a curious house with eight sides. The troubled times halted its completion, but it remains with one story finished.

North of Natchez stands Emerald Mound, built by Indians as a

The Meridian Naval Air Station is a training base for jet pilots.

base for temples. Nearby is the Homochitto National Forest, 189,072 acres (76,515 hectares) of shady woodland famous for fishing, hunting, and camping.

In east-central Mississippi lies Meridian, a growing industrial, commercial, and agricultural center. A naval air station there is a training base for jet pilots.

Hattiesburg, at the edge of the vast De Soto National Forest, is a producer of lumber and naval stores. The University of Southern Mississippi, with about 11,600 students, is located there.

GULF COAST MISSISSIPPI

The subtropical Gulf Coast of Mississippi is not only one of America's outstanding resort areas, but is also a thriving area for shipping, marine construction, and manufacturing.

In the extreme southeast corner of Mississippi lies thriving Pascagoula, one of the nation's great shipbuilding centers. Its

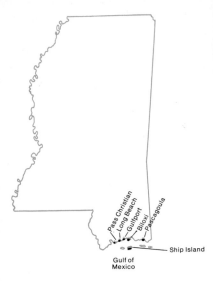

Fort Massachusetts, on Ship Island, was a Union stronghold.

history began with the building of the Old Spanish Fort in the early 1700s. Actually, the fort was constructed by the French, but the Spanish later captured it. The fort's sturdy walls are made of massive pine trunks cemented with oyster shells, moss, and mud. It is thought to be the oldest building in the Mississippi Valley.

A local mystery involves the Pascagoula River, which makes a strange humming sound. According to legend, the son of a Pascagoula Indian chieftain longed to marry a princess of the neighboring Biloxi tribe. This infuriated the Biloxi ruler, who attacked the Pascagoula. Knowing they could not withstand the onslaught, the Pascagoula joined hands and marched singing into the river to drown. It is said that their singing is what visitors hear today.

Largest and oldest of the coastal cities is Biloxi, which was settled in 1699. The first settlers were Frenchmen, and to encourage them to stay, eighty girls were carefully selected by a bishop in France and sent to the new colony as brides. The young ladies landed at Ship Island, near Biloxi, where much later Fort Massachusetts was built as a Union stronghold.

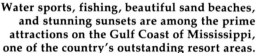
Water sports, fishing, beautiful sand beaches, and stunning sunsets are among the prime attractions on the Gulf Coast of Mississippi, one of the country's outstanding resort areas.

Biloxi has been a popular resort since the mid-1800s. Crepe myrtle, roses, camellias, and magnolias beautify Biloxi's streets and Spanish moss festoons the oaks. Boats ply the harbor, and there is year-round freshwater, saltwater, and deep-sea fishing.

The Biloxi Lighthouse towers above the seashore. When Biloxi was threatened by a Union invasion in the Civil War, a man climbed to the top, removed the lens of the light, and buried it for safekeeping. The tower was painted black when Biloxi learned of the assassination of Abraham Lincoln.

Lincoln's greatest opponent, Jefferson Davis, spent the last years of his life at Biloxi in a colonnaded house called Beauvoir.

Many visitors take a boat excursion to Ship Island. A beautiful spot is Deer Island, the legendary hiding place of pirate treasure, much talked about but never actually found.

Perhaps Biloxi's prime attraction for vacationers is the Harrison County Sand Beach, a strip of white sand that stretches for miles along the Gulf, the world's longest artificially created beach.

West of Biloxi is Gulfport, a planned city with broad and regular streets. Gulfport is a major rail and shipping center. Although the city was built with only shipping in mind, it became a resort in the 1920s and is part of "America's Riviera."

A large number of the bananas that appear in the nation's markets pass through Gulfport. The mechanized banana terminal can handle 9,600 banana stems—huge bunches—in an hour.

Just off Gulfport is a dot of land called Cat Island. Cat Island, despite its name, became the place where the United States Army trained K-9 Corps war dogs in World War II. A joke at the time was that Cat Island had gone to the dogs.

Just west of Gulfport lies Long Beach, a town blessed with five miles (eight kilometers) of gulf-front beach. Long Beach is a resort town that dates back to an Indian trading post established more than 250 years ago.

A few miles farther west is Pass Christian (*Pass Christy-Ann* according to the French pronunciation). The South's earliest yacht club was established there in 1849. Harbor Park is an attractive recreation area with tennis courts, a baseball diamond, a playground, and a marina for boating and deep-sea fishing.

Near Bay St. Louis, on the southwest Gulf Coast, is the National Space Technology Laboratory (NSTL) and Earth Resources Laboratory. This NASA installation was once used mainly as a testing site for space-shuttle engines, but now concentrates on ecology and earth-science research.

From the days when King Cotton ruled the Old South to the space-age technology of the New South, the Magnolia State has made a steady advance toward its goal of better education, new industries, better jobs, and better lives for all Mississippians.

FACTS AT A GLANCE

GENERAL INFORMATION

Statehood: December 10, 1817, twentieth state

Origin of Name: Mississippi takes its name from the Mississippi River, which forms much of its western boundary. Mississippi is a Choctaw Indian word meaning *Great Water* or *Father of Waters.*

State Capital: Jackson, founded 1821

State Nickname: The Magnolia State

State Flag: Mississippi's state flag, adopted in 1894, reflects its membership in the Confederacy and in the United States. The upper left, or canton, corner contains the Confederate battle flag—thirteen white stars within two diagonal blue bars, those bars bordered by white lines. The stars and bars lie in a red field. The rest of the flag contains three broad horizontal bars of blue, white, and red, the colors of the American flag.

State Motto: *Virtute et Armis*, Latin words meaning "By valor and arms"

State Bird: Mockingbird

State Water Fowl: Wood duck

State Fish: Largemouth bass

State Insect: Honeybee

State Land Mammal: White-tailed deer

State Water Mammal: Bottle-nosed dolphin

State Stone: Petrified wood

State Flower: Magnolia blossom

State Tree: Magnolia

State Song: "Go, Mississippi," words and music by Houston Davis, adopted as the state song in 1962:

Verse:

          States may sing their songs of praise
          With waving flags and hip-hoo-rays,
          Let cymbals crash and let bells ring
          'Cause here's one song I'm proud to sing.

Choruses:

          Go, Mississippi, keep rolling along,
          Go, Mississippi, you cannot go wrong,
          Go, Mississippi, we're singing your song,
          M-I-S-S-I-S-S-I-P-P-I

          Go, Mississippi, you're on the right track,
          Go, Mississippi, and this is a fact,
          Go, Mississippi, you'll never look back,
          M-I-S-S-I-S-S-I-P-P-I

          Go, Mississippi, straight down the line,
          Go, Mississippi, ev'rything's fine,
          Go, Mississippi, it's your state and mine,
          M-I-S-S-I-S-S-I-P-P-I

          Go, Mississippi, continue to roll,
          Go, Mississippi, the top is the goal,
          Go, Mississippi, you'll have and you'll hold,
          M-I-S-S-I-S-S-I-P-P-I

          Go, Mississippi, get up and go,
          Go, Mississippi, let the world know,
          That our Mississippi is leading the show,
          M-I-S-S-I-S-S-I-P-P-I

POPULATION

Population: 2,573,216, thirty-first among the states (1990 census)

Population Density: 54.9 people per sq. mi. (21.2 per km²)

Population Distribution: 53 percent rural, 47 percent urban. The four major metropolitan areas are Jackson, Gulfport-Biloxi, Greenville, and Hattiesburg.

Jackson	196,637
Biloxi	46,319
Greenville	45,226
Hattiesburg	41,882
Meridian	41,036

```
Gulfport. . . . . . . . . . . . . . . . . . . . . . . . . . . . . . . . . . . . . . . . . .   40,775
Tupelo . . . . . . . . . . . . . . . . . . . . . . . . . . . . . . . . . . . . . . . . . .   30,685
Pascagoula . . . . . . . . . . . . . . . . . . . . . . . . . . . . . . . . . . . . . .   25,899
Columbus . . . . . . . . . . . . . . . . . . . . . . . . . . . . . . . . . . . . . . .   23,799
Vicksburg . . . . . . . . . . . . . . . . . . . . . . . . . . . . . . . . . . . . . . .   20,908
Clinton. . . . . . . . . . . . . . . . . . . . . . . . . . . . . . . . . . . . . . . . . .   19,717
```
(Population figures according to 1990 census)

Population Growth: Mississippi's population grew continuously until World War I, when the rate of growth tapered off slightly. The population reached a peak in 1930. The migration of blacks to northern cities slowed or reversed Mississippi's population growth between 1930 and 1970. Protection under the civil-rights laws of the 1960s and new job opportunities in the 1970s slowed this migration. Mississippi's population increased 2.1 percent between 1980 and 1990; during this time, the population of the entire country grew 9.8 percent. The list below shows population growth in Mississippi since 1820; the figures for 1820, 1840, and 1860 do not include blacks who were slaves.

Year	Population
1820	75,448
1840	375,651
1860	791,305
1880	1,131,597
1900	1,551,270
1920	1,790,618
1930	2,009,821
1940	2,183,796
1950	2,178,914
1960	2,178,141
1970	2,216,994
1980	2,520,638
1990	2,573,216

GEOGRAPHY

Borders: States that border Mississippi are Louisiana and Arkansas on the west, Tennessee on the north, and Alabama on the east. The Gulf of Mexico forms Mississippi's southern border.

Highest Point: Woodall Mountain, 806 ft. (246 m) above sea level

Lowest Point: Sea level, along the coast of the Gulf of Mexico

Greatest Distances: North to south—340 mi. (563 km)
East to west—142 mi. (228 km)

Area: 47,716 sq. mi. (123,583 km²)

Rank in Area Among the States: Thirty-second

Catching succulent crabs on St. Louis Bay (above) and other areas along the Gulf Coast is a popular pastime.

Rivers: A number of major rivers and dozens of minor ones provide Mississippi with an excellent drainage system. The Mississippi River flows for 2,348 mi. (3,779 km) through the heart of the United States and forms most of Mississippi's western border. Two other large rivers, the Yazoo and Big Black, lie entirely within the state and flow into the Mississippi. The Pearl and Pascagoula rivers flow in the eastern part of Mississippi to the Gulf of Mexico. Another important river, the Tombigbee (525 mi./845 km), crosses the northeastern corner of Mississippi on its way from Tennessee to Alabama. Northern Mississippi also has the Tallahatchie River.

Lakes: The largest lakes in Mississippi are artificial. Dams built to control floods have formed long, narrow reservoirs that serve as lakes. Among the largest of these artificial lakes is the Ross Barnett Reservoir, which provides water and recreation near Jackson. Four other reservoirs—the Grenada, Arkabutla, Enid, and Sardis—form lakes in the northern part of the state. Mississippi also contains many oxbow lakes (named after their shape). These lakes were once bends in the river and were left isolated when the river changed course. Southern Mississippi has many bayous—marshy, slow-moving bodies of water.

Coasts: A 44-mi. (71-km) coastline forms the state's southern border. The coast, with its bays, inlets, and offshore islands, gives Mississippi 359 mi. (578 km) of shoreline. At Bay St. Louis, America's largest seawall protects the shore between Biloxi and Point Henderson.

Topography: Mississippi consists of two main regions, which have been determined by its rivers. The soils found in each region helped determine the character of that region.

The western edge of the state is described as the Alluvial Plain. It covers a triangular-shaped area in the northwest region of the state and includes a thin strip of land south of Vicksburg. Mississippians call this region the Yazoo Basin or the Delta. Thousands of years of flooding by the Mississippi and its tributaries have deposited rich, black soil in this area. Farmers used this fertile soil to grow cotton and later, soybeans.

The eastern part of Mississippi, the East Gulf Coast Plain, holds much more variety. A finger of land called the Black Belt reaches into eastern Mississippi. The Black Belt, named for its rich soil, is well suited to farming. Much of the Gulf Coast Plain is thin-soiled land, better suited for livestock grazing than for farming. Prairies and woodlands dot this eastern region. The south-central section, covered by evergreens, is known as the Piney Woods. Small hills may be found throughout the Gulf Coast Plain, but the hills become larger in the northeast. Woodall Mountain, in the northeast corner, is the highest point in the state.

Climate: Summer temperatures average 82° F. (28° C), but temperatures of 90° F. to 95° F. (32° C to 35° C) are common. Winter temperatures are warm by other states' standards, with average January temperatures of 48° F. (9° C). The mild winters provide growing seasons of 180 to 200 days in northern Mississippi, 250 to 300 days in the south. The record high temperature was 115° F. (46° C) at Holly Springs on July 9, 1830. The lowest recorded Mississippi temperature was -19° F. (-28° C) at Corinth on January 30, 1966. Precipitation ranges from 50 in. (127 cm) in the north to 65 in. (165 cm) in the south. Snow is rare and seldom remains long. Natural disasters sometimes strike. Tornadoes may ravage Mississippi during the late spring. Hurricanes may wreak havoc on the Gulf Coast during late summer and early fall. Despite the many levees and dams, the Mississippi River occasionally overflows and causes millions of dollars worth of damage.

NATURE

Trees: Forests cover about 56 percent of Mississippi's land area. More than a hundred varieties of trees can be found, including magnolia, pine, pecan, oak, cottonwood, hickory, tupelo, sweet gum, dogwood, and bald cypress.

Wild Plants: Azaleas, camellias, redbuds, violets, black-eyed Susans, mountain laurels, dogwood, and Cherokee roses are among the hundreds of flowers in Mississippi. Many shrubs, wildflowers, and grasses flourish throughout the state.

Animals: Deer, foxes, mink, woodchucks, beavers, muskrats, squirrels, rabbits, opossums, raccoons, and skunks are found throughout the state.

Birds: Mockingbirds, doves, ducks, and quail are among the birds that live in Mississippi throughout the year. Many birds make seasonal stopovers in Mississippi during their migrations north or south.

Fish: Catfish, bass, bream, crappie, buffalo carp, and perch are among Mississippi's freshwater fish. Deep-sea fishermen try their luck at landing tarpon, drum, sheephead, flounder, mackerel, menhaden, and redfish. Shellfish such as oysters and shrimp also may be found.

GOVERNMENT

Mississippi state government, like the federal government, is divided into executive, legislative, and judicial branches. The governor heads the executive branch, which is responsible for enforcing laws and administering the state's business. The governor approves or vetoes laws proposed by the legislature and may call special sessions of the legislature. The governor is elected to a four-year term, and according to a 1986 constitutional amendment may serve two successive terms. The executive branch also includes a lieutenant governor, secretary of state, attorney general, auditor, and treasurer. These officials also are elected to four-year terms.

The legislative branch, which is responsible for making laws, meets each year for 90 to 125 days. The legislature may also override a governor's veto of a proposed law and may propose amendments to the state constitution. Mississippi's legislature consists of a senate, which has 52 members, and a house of representatives, which has 122 members. Legislators are elected to four-year terms.

The judicial branch of the government has the responsibility and the power to interpret laws. The highest judicial authority rests with the state supreme court, which is composed of nine judges elected from three different districts. Each justice serves an eight-year term. Mississippi's judicial branch also includes circuit courts, which hear criminal and civil cases, and chancery courts, which hear civil cases. Judges of these courts serve four-year terms.

Number of Counties: 82

U.S. Representatives: 5

Electoral Votes: 7

Voting Qualifications: United States citizen, eighteen years of age, and must be registered to vote at least thirty days before an election.

EDUCATION

Mississippi has more than 12,000 public elementary and secondary schools. These schools serve about 505,550 students. Nearly 50,000 attend private schools. Public schools are controlled by a nine-person state board of education. Five of those members are chosen by the governor, two by the lieutenant governor, and two by the secretary of state. The board of education selects a state school superintendent who is responsible for the curriculum and control of the schools.

Mississippi has forty-six institutions of higher learning, including sixteen public and private colleges and universities. The largest three are public schools: Southern Mississippi, located in Hattiesburg, serves about 11,600 students; Mississippi State University, near Starkville, serves about 13,300; the University of Mississippi, at Oxford, serves about 10,000. Other state-run schools include Delta State, in Cleveland; Mississippi University for Women, in Columbus; Alcorn State, in Lorman; Jackson State, in Jackson; and Mississippi Valley State, in Itta Bena; these last three have mostly black enrollments. Prominent church-run schools include Blue Mountain College in Blue Mountain, William Carey College in Hattiesburg, and Mississippi College in Clinton (Baptist); Millsaps College in Jackson and Rust College in Holly Springs (Methodist); and Bellhaven College in Jackson (Presbyterian). Tougaloo College, in Tougaloo, is a privately endowed institution.

For many years, the policy of racial segregation played a major role in Mississippi education: there were separate schools for white children and black children. Racial separation was practiced in 1870 when the first public schools opened; separation was made mandatory by Mississippi's 1890 constitution. The enforced separation diluted the already meager school funds. As a result, Mississippi had one of the nation's poorest and least-effective school systems. The United States Supreme Court ordered integration in 1954, but Mississippi's government continued to resist. A compulsory school-attendance law, originally passed in 1918, was repealed in 1956 in an attempt to prevent forced integration. When public schools began to integrate in 1964, many whites opened private schools so that white children could avoid contact with black children. In time, those "segregation academies" declined in importance. All of Mississippi's public schools have been integrated since 1970, and as of 1981, fewer than 10 percent of school-aged children attended private schools. Compulsory school attendance for those aged six to thirteen was reinstated in 1982. In 1982, the Mississippi legislature passed the Education Reform Act, designed to improve the state's public-school system. The Reform Act has become a model program for education.

ECONOMY AND INDUSTRY

Principal Products:
Agriculture: Cotton, soybeans, beef cattle, broiler chickens, milk, eggs, rice, cottonseed, sweet potatoes, farm-raised catfish
Manufacturing: Transportation equipment, electric machinery and equipment, lumber and wood products, food products, clothing, chemicals, nonelectric machinery, paper products, fabricated metal products, furniture and fixtures, stone, clay, and glass products
Fishing Industry: Menhaden, shrimp, red snapper, and oysters
Natural Resources: Petroleum, natural gas, sand, gravel, clay, soil, large forests, abundant water from rivers

Business and Trade: Mississippi has more than 14,000 retail establishments and more than 3,500 wholesale centers. Jackson, the state capital, is also its business center. Service industries make up most of Jackson's trade. Other cities serve as trading hubs for various products. Greenwood, Aberdeen, Grenada, and Clarksdale are important cotton markets. Yazoo City and Tupelo are regional livestock centers. Vicksburg has a busy lumber market. Gulfport and Biloxi serve as shipping centers for lumber, cotton, and seafood.

Finance: More than 100 state banks with 450 branches are located in Mississippi. In addition, there are about 30 national banks with about 300 branches. The state also has 30 savings and loan associations and 13 savings banks.

Communication: Mississippi has about 120 newspapers, 22 of which are dailies, as well as 40 periodicals. Major newspapers include the Jackson *Clarion-Ledger* and *Jackson Daily News*, Biloxi's *Daily Herald/The Sun*, the *Meridian Star*, the *Hattiesburg American*, Tupelo's *Northeast Mississippi Daily Journal*, Greenville's *Delta Democrat-Times*, and Pascagoula's *Mississippi Press*. Mississippi also has 179 radio stations and 18 television stations.

Transportation: Mississippi, a major crossroad of the South, has one of the South's best highway systems. The state has 10,900 mi. (17,542 km) of roads and streets, including 680 mi. (1,094 km) of highways that are part of the interstate highway system. Mississippi has about 160 airports, including 12 major ones. About 3,500 mi. (5,633 km) of railroad track crisscross the state.

Mississippi has one of America's most important water-transportation systems. Two deep-water seaports, Gulfport and Pascagoula, handle about 20 million tons (18 million metric tons) of goods per year. Biloxi is another important Gulf of Mexico port. The Mississippi River is an important inland waterway, and Greenville, Natchez, and Vicksburg are major Mississippi River ports. Other rivers, including the Pearl and Yazoo, also carry extensive traffic. The Tennessee-Tombigbee Waterway connects the Tennessee and Tombigbee rivers and provides the northeastern part of the state with access to the Gulf of Mexico.

SOCIAL AND CULTURAL LIFE

Museums: Mississippi is home to a number of fine museums, most of which deal with the state and the South. The State Historical Museum in Jackson contains Indian relics, a copy of Mississippi's Ordinance of Secession, and a hall of fame. Jackson also hosts the Mississippi Museum of Natural Science, which contains dioramas showing the ecological history of the state. The Lauren Rogers Museum of Art in Laurel contains many paintings by American, French, and British masters, plus a noted collection of baskets. The Kate Shipworth Teaching Museum at the University of Mississippi is known for its collection of classical archaeology. Cottonlandia in Greenwood is a museum devoted to cotton. Other Mississippi museums include the Mississippi Museum of Art, in Jackson; the Mary Buie Art Museum, in Oxford; the Delta Blues Museum, at Clarksdale; and the Old Court House Museum, at Vicksburg. The Russell C. Davis Planetarium, in Jackson, offers astronomy shows and starlight concerts. The Mississippi Agricultural and Forestry Museum, in Jackson, has delighted young people for years.

The Old Court House Museum at Vicksburg, once bombarded by Union gunboats, houses displays of material on the Confederacy.

Libraries: The first public library in Mississippi was established in Port Gibson in 1818. Now, more than 250 public libraries, governed by a well-financed library commission, serve the state. Mississippi has a number of important private libraries. The University of Mississippi houses a fine collection of works by Mississippi writers William Faulkner and Stark Young. It also houses the Center for the Study of Southern Culture, a research center of southern music, folklore, and literature. Mississippi State University is the custodian of the papers of longtime United States senator John Stennis. The Mississippi Department of Archives in Jackson preserves an extensive collection of documents dealing with Mississippi and United States history. The State Law Library in Jackson has a large collection of law documents. Southern Mississippi University's library contains a huge collection of original illustrations and manuscripts of children's books.

Performing Arts: Most people associate Mississippi with country music as well as blues, partly because Mississippi is the home of so many world-famous stars of those musical fields. But the state also has strong classical music programs. Five symphony orchestras are located here, the oldest in Jackson. Many college groups throughout Mississippi also offer classical performances. Jackson hosts the Mississippi Opera Association, which has pioneered opera in the state.

Ever since showboats took minstrel shows from town to town along the river, Mississippians have enjoyed theater performances. The Dixie Showboat Players in Vicksburg offer lively variety shows. The Jackson Little Theater (now called New Stage), founded in 1925, is one of the oldest such groups in the country. More than twenty other theater companies flourish throughout the state.

Sports and Recreation: College sports, especially football, draw widespread interest in Mississippi. The University of Mississippi (Ole Miss) was a longtime powerhouse of the Southeastern Conference. In recent times, Mississippi State University and Southern Mississippi University have developed strong football programs. Mississippians play tennis and golf throughout the year. The Magnolia Open Golf Classic in Hattiesburg draws top-ranked golf professionals each April. Another popular event is Gulfport's Deep Sea Fishing Rodeo held every July.

Jackson's zoo is one of the most popular attractions in the state. It contains about four hundred species of animals and birds in simulated natural environments. Mynelle Gardens, also in Jackson, is a bird sanctuary with hundreds of colorful flowers and shrubs. One of the state's major tourist draws is the Gulf Coast beach between Henderson Point and Biloxi—the nation's longest artificially created beach.

Outdoor lovers find a wealth of activities in Mississippi. The state has twenty-six state parks, which protect woods, wildlife refuges, lakes, bayous, and beaches. De Soto, Bienville, Delta, Holly Springs, and Homochitto national forests offer camping and hiking facilities.

Historic Sites and Landmarks:

Ackia Battlefield, near Tupelo, was the site of an important 1736 battle between the French and the Chickasaw Indians. With the help of the English, the Chickasaw Indians routed the French and prevented them from securing a base in the Mississippi Valley.

Beauvoir, near Biloxi, is an antebellum mansion that was the last home of Jefferson Davis. After the war, it became a home for Confederate war veterans and their wives.

Brice's Cross Roads National Battlefield, near Baldwyn, marks a major Confederate Civil War victory. Southern troops led by Nathan Bedford Forrest were outnumbered 8,000 to 3,500, yet they drove the Union troops back and captured most of the Union artillery.

Cairo Gunboat, in Vicksburg, is a restored iron-clad gunboat that also contains a time capsule of Civil War artifacts.

Connelly's Tavern, in Natchez, an inn built along the old Natchez Trace, was at one time the last outpost on the southwestern frontier of America.

Cross and Boulder, near Biloxi, marks the site of an early French landing in Mississippi.

Emerald Mound, built by a now-vanished Indian tribe, spreads over 8 acres (3.2 hectares) near Washington, a few miles east of Natchez.

Florewood River Plantation, near Greenwood, includes twenty-two buildings and shows what life was like on a nineteenth-century cotton plantation.

Rosalie is one of the many beautiful antebellum mansions in Natchez.

Fort Massachusetts, on Ship Island, was built on the orders of Jefferson Davis when he was United States secretary of war. Early in the Civil War, Confederate forces captured and partially destroyed it. Union troops later rebuilt the fort and used it as a prison for Confederate soldiers.

Friendship Cemetery, in Columbus, was the site of the first Memorial Day. Women from the town decorated graves of both Union and Confederate soldiers here in 1866.

Jefferson College, in Washington, was the state's first institution of higher learning. It was also the site of Aaron Burr's treason arraignment in 1807. Burr had been charged with trying to form his own nation in the Southwest.

Longwood, in Natchez, is a mansion known for its onion-top dome and unusual eight-sided architectural style. Its construction was interrupted by the Civil War, and the home was never completed.

Old Capitol, in Jackson, was built in Greek Revival style. It is now the State Historical Museum.

Old Spanish Fort, in Pascagoula, built in the early 1700s, is considered the oldest structure still standing in the Mississippi River Valley. French, British, Spanish, Confederate, and American flags have flown over this fort.

Rosalie, in Natchez, one of many beautiful antebellum mansions in the area, was built in 1820. Union troops occupied it and used it as a headquarters during the Civil War.

Tupelo National Battlefield, near Tupelo, was the site of the 1864 Battle of Tupelo. Confederate troops led by Stephen D. Lee and Nathan Bedford Forrest were routed here, in one of Mississippi's last Civil War battles.

Vicksburg National Military Park, in Vicksburg, preserves reminders of the 1863 siege that gave Union forces control of the Mississippi River. The park contains remains of trenches, gun emplacements, and rifle pits used by the Confederate defenders. The nearby cemetery holds graves of more than eighteen thousand soldiers. A monument from each Confederate and Union state honors the soldiers of both sides who fought the Battle of Vicksburg.

Other Interesting Places to Visit:

Biloxi Lighthouse was built in 1848 and painted black after the Civil War by Mississippians who mourned the death of Abraham Lincoln. It has been repainted its original white color.

Blues Archives, at the University of Mississippi in Oxford, has a large collection of blues recordings, including nine thousand B.B. King records.

Elvis Presley's Birthplace, in Tupelo on the grounds of Elvis Presley Park, is a modest house open to the public.

Friendship Oak, in Pass Christian, is believed by scientists to date from 1487. Mississippi legend says that those who pass under its shadow remain lifelong friends.

Governor's Mansion, in Jackson, was completed in 1841. It contains many antiques and period pieces. In 1972, the mansion was renovated under the direction of then first lady Carroll Waller.

Natchez Trace Parkway is a scenic drive along the old Natchez Trace. This trace, between Nashville, Tennessee, and Natchez, Mississippi, was the most heavily traveled road in the Southeast between 1800 and 1820. Flatboatmen floated south down the Mississippi River to Natchez and New Orleans where they sold their boats as well as their cargos, and then hiked home along the trace.

Ocean Springs, a picturesque Gulf Coast town, is a thriving colony of artists and craftspeople. It hosts a spring festival each April.

Petrified Forest, near Flora, contains giant stone trees, a geological museum, a rock and gem shop, and picnic areas.

Rowan Oak, in Oxford, was the home where prize-winning author William Faulkner wrote many of his novels. It is now owned by the University of Mississippi and serves as a museum.

The Biloxi Lighthouse, built in 1848, contains an exhibit of its history.

Waterways Experiment Station, in Vicksburg, run by the United States Army Corps of Engineers, has a model of the lower Mississippi River Valley. Engineers use the model to simulate flood conditions in hope of finding solutions to flooding problems.

IMPORTANT DATES

800 B.C.-A.D. 1000 — Indian farmers begin growing corn, squash, and tobacco and learn the art of making pottery

1050-1650 — Mississippian culture flourishes; mounds built

1541 — Spanish explorer Hernando De Soto finds the Mississippi River

1682 — French explorer René-Robert Cavelier, Sieur de La Salle, claims the Mississippi River Valley for France and names it Louisiana in honor of King Louis XIV

1698 — English traders begin to barter with the local Chickasaw Indians

1699 — French trader Pierre Le Moyne, Sieur d'Iberville, founds Mississippi's first settlement at Old Biloxi (now Ocean Springs)

1717—Scottish adventurer John Law, with permission from the French regent, opens a land company and lures many investors to undeveloped Mississippi with false promises, causing a financial panic when the investors sell their worthless stock

1719—The French import the first African slaves to work on rice and tobacco plantations

1736—Chickasaw Indians, aided by the British, defeat the French at the Battle of Ackia and weaken the French position in North America

1763—The British defeat the French and gain control of Mississippi after the French and Indian War

1763-1779—The British rule Mississippi as part of the colony called West Florida

1779—Spaniards take over West Florida

1783—The Treaty of Paris sets United States southern boundary at 31st parallel

1795—The United States gains much of West Florida from Spain, although the Spaniards still control the Gulf Coast

1798—Congress organizes the Mississippi Territory—land from the Mississippi River to the Chattahoochee River—although most of northern Mississippi is still Indian territory; Natchez becomes territorial capital

1800—Andrew Marschalk publishes the *Mississippi Gazette*, first newspaper in the territory

1801—The Choctaw and Chickasaw Indians give the United States permission to build the Natchez Trace, a trail from Nashville, Tennessee, to Natchez, Mississippi

1802—Capital of the territory is transferred from Natchez six miles east to Washington

1803—The United States buys the Louisiana Territory from the French, assuring Mississippi Territory residents free trade and safe immigration along the territory's western border

1804—Congress extends Mississippi Territory north to the Tennessee border (the 35th parallel)

1806—Introduction of an improved variety of cotton, using seeds imported from Mexico, helps cotton become "King" in Mississippi

1807—Aaron Burr arrested in Washington, Mississippi, for treason, amid rumors that he was conspiring to establish a separate republic in the Southwest

1810—President James Madison sends forces to Spanish West Florida when settlers secede and declare their independence from Spain

1811—Jefferson College, Mississippi's first college, opens

1812—The section of West Florida between the Pearl and Perdido rivers (below the 31st parallel) is added to Mississippi Territory

1817—Congress divides Mississippi Territory; western half admitted to the Union as the state of Mississippi, eastern half becomes Alabama Territory

1819—Elizabeth Female Academy, the state's first school for women, opens in Washington

1821—Legislature chooses a site on Le Fleur's Bluff for new state capital; Franklin Academy, Mississippi's first public school, opens in Columbus

1822—Legislature meets in newly built capital of Jackson, named after Andrew Jackson, a hero of the War of 1812

1830—Choctaw representatives sign a treaty at Dancing Rabbit Creek, agreeing to trade their Mississippi River lands for land in little-known Oklahoma

1832—Chickasaw representatives cede their Mississippi territories in return for land in Oklahoma

1848—University of Mississippi opens

1858—Legislation sets up a board of levee commissioners; much of Mississippi's swampland is drained and made suitable for farming

1861—Mississippi secedes from the Union, joins other southern states in Confederate States of America; Mississippian Jefferson Davis is named president of the Confederacy

1863—Emancipation Proclamation declares all remaining Mississippi slaves free; Vicksburg falls to Union forces after a long siege, giving the Union control of the Mississippi River

1866—Women at Columbus decorate graves of Union and Confederate soldiers, in what becomes the first Memorial Day

1868—"Black and Tan" convention of white and black delegates creates a new constitution that allows Mississippi blacks to vote and hold office

1870—United States military rule ends, with Mississippi readmitted to the Union; Chinese first come to Mississippi; the Indian Removal Act eventually causes Chickasaw and Choctaw Indians remaining in Mississippi to be swept up in the forced march to Oklahoma known as the Trail of Tears

1871—Alcorn University established as the first state-supported college for blacks in United States

1875—"Bourbon Democrats" gain control of the legislature, impeach Republican governor Adelbert Ames and lieutenant-governor A. K. Davis

1878—Mississippi A&M College (now Mississippi State University) is founded

1884—Mississippi University for Women, the nation's first state-supported school for women, opens

1890—Mississippi adopts a new constitution that revokes many rights extended to blacks under the previous constitution

1903—New capitol is completed

1904—Legislature creates textbook commission in charge of buying all schoolbooks in the state

1906—Rural schools are established

1907—The boll weevil, an insect that destroys cotton, first appears in Mississippi; weevils soon cause damage amounting to millions of dollars

1908—Mississippi creates its first agricultural high schools

1912—Mississippi passes laws regulating child labor

1918—A large number of blacks begin leaving Mississippi, taking the Illinois Central railroad north for better jobs and improved civil rights

1927—Heavy floods swamp the Delta, leaving 100,000 homeless and forcing nearly 200,000 persons to flee

1936—In a move to diversify the economy, Mississippi adopts the BAWI program (Balance Agriculture With Industry)—special laws to encourage manufacturing

1939—Oil is discovered at Tinsley in Yazoo County

1948—Southern Democrats form States Rights, or Dixiecrat, party; Governor Fielding Wright selected as vice-presidential candidate

1949—William Faulkner, Mississippi's most famous author, wins the Nobel Prize in literature

1962—James Meredith enters the University of Mississippi as its first black student, despite protests from Governor Ross Barnett; resulting riots leave two people dead; President John F. Kennedy sends federal troops to establish and maintain order

1964—Integration comes to Mississippi's elementary and high schools; education again becomes compulsory for children ages six to thirteen; Barry Goldwater captures Mississippi's electoral votes, becoming the first Republican presidential candidate to do so

1968—A largely black "freedom" delegation of Mississippi Democrats succeeds in having its delegation recognized by the Democratic national convention

1969—Charles Evers elected mayor of Fayette, becoming first black mayor of a racially mixed city

1970—Two students are killed by police at Jackson State University

1973—Eudora Welty wins Pulitzer Prize in fiction for *The Optimist's Daughter*

1985—The Tennessee-Tombigbee Waterway opens, providing direct shipping from the Tennessee River to the Gulf of Mexico

1986—Mike Espy becomes Mississippi's first black congressman since 1883

1988—Biloxi native Eugene A. Marino is named the nation's first black Roman Catholic archbishop

1989—Governor Ray Mabus announces an education reform package designed to provide Mississippi children with a world-class education by the year 2000

1990—Governor Mabus was named one of the top ten education governors by *Fortune* magazine

1992—Kirk Fordice becomes the first Republican governor of Mississippi since 1876

1994—Byron de la Beckwith is convicted of the 1963 murder of Medgar Evers

IMPORTANT PEOPLE

Dana Andrews (1912-1992), born in Collins; actor; starred in the films *A Walk in the Sun* and *The Best Years of Our Lives*

Sherwood Bonner (1849-1883), born Katherine Sherwood, full name Katherine Sherwood Bonner McDowell; as a young girl lived in Holly Springs; wrote short story collections *Dialect Tales* and *Suwanee River Tales* and the novel *Like Unto Like*, which described the Civil War and Reconstruction periods

Ralph Boston (1939-   ), born in Laurel; track-and-field star; won a gold medal and set Olympic long-jump record for United States in 1960 with jump of 26 feet, 7 3/4 inches

DANA ANDREWS

BLANCHE BRUCE

HODDING CARTER II

MART CROWLEY

BO DIDDLEY

William ("Big Bill") Broonzy (1893-1958), born in Scott; musician; became one of the giants of country-blues music; influenced Pete Seeger, Sonny Terry, and Brownie McGee; wrote the songs "Too Too Train Blues" and "Worrying You off My Mind"

Albert Gallatin Brown (1813-1880), politician; governor (1844-48); worked for free public schools and popular election of judges

Blanche K. Bruce (1841-1898), politician; first black to serve a full term as U.S. senator (1875-81)

Hodding Carter II (1907-1972), journalist and novelist; won the 1946 Pulitzer Prize as publisher of the *Delta Democrat-Times* for his editorials advocating religious and racial tolerance

Will Clark (1964-   ), professional baseball player; All-American baseball player at Mississippi State University; a star of the 1984 U.S. Olympic exhibition baseball team; led the 1987 San Francisco Giants to the National League West championship

Thad Cochran (1937-   ), born in Pontotoc; politician; first Republican congressman (elected in 1972) and senator (elected in 1978) in Mississippi since Reconstruction

Charles Conerly (1921-   ), born in Clarksdale; professional football player; quarterback at University of Mississippi (1945-47); elected to College Football Hall of Fame; led New York Giants to four division titles between 1948 and 1961

Mart Crowley (1935-   ), born in Vicksburg; playwright; wrote *The Boys in the Band*, which ran more than 1,000 performances on Broadway

Jefferson Davis (1808-1889), army officer, politician; commanded first Mississippi regiment in Mexican War; U.S. representative (1845-46); U.S. senator (1847-51); secretary of war (1853-57); President of the Confederate States of America (1861-65); wrote *The Rise and Fall of the Confederate Government* (1881)

Hernando De Soto (1500?-1542), Spanish explorer who discovered Mississippi River; first European to set foot in Mississippi

Bo Diddley (1928-   ), born Elias McDaniels in McComb; singer and guitar player who became one of the first rock-and-roll stars with songs such as "Bo Diddley" and "Who Do You Love?"

William Dunbar (1749-1810), scientist and writer; improved the cotton gin and discovered the value of cottonseed oil; explored Mississippi and wrote about its wildlife

Mike Espy (1953-   ), born in Yazoo City; first black congressman from Mississippi (1986) since 1883; secretary of agriculture (1993-94)

Charles Evers (1922-   ), born in Decatur; civil-rights leader; mayor of Fayette (1969-81), the first black mayor elected to lead a racially mixed southern city

Medgar Wiley Evers (1925-1963), born in Decatur; NAACP field secretary and civil-rights leader murdered in Mississippi while leading a civil-rights demonstration

William Faulkner (1897-1962), born in New Albany; author; often considered the greatest American novelist of the twentieth century; spent most of his literary career working in Oxford, writing about imaginary Yoknapatawpha County; received the 1949 Nobel Prize in literature, the 1949 Pulitzer Prize in fiction for *A Fable*, and the 1963 Pulitzer Prize in fiction for *The Reivers*

Henry S. Foote (1800-1880), politician; governor (1852-54)

Shelby Foote (1916-   ), born in Greenville; historian and novelist; best known for a three-volume history of the Civil War and *Shiloh*

SHELBY FOOTE

Ruth Ford (1915-   ), born in Brookhaven; actress of stage and screen; starred in Broadway plays *Six Characters in Search of an Author* and *Dinner at Eight*

Nathan Bedford Forrest (1821-1877), Confederate general; best known for his daring raids; won Battle of Brice's Cross Roads although outnumbered more than two to one by Union troops

Bobbie Gentry (1944-   ), born in Chickasaw County; singer whose ballad "Ode to Billy Joe" was the best-selling song of 1967

RUTH FORD

James Zachariah George (1826-1897), jurist and legislator; chief justice of Mississippi State Supreme Court; considered the "father of the department of agriculture"; played major role in creating Sherman Anti-Trust Act in 1890

Fannie Lou Hamer (1917-1977), born in Mississippi; civil-rights leader; one of founders of Freedom Democratic party that challenged whites in 1970s

Barry Hannah (1943-   ), author; grew up in Clinton; wrote *Geronimo Rex* and *Airships*

NATHAN FORREST

Jim Henson (1936-1990), born in Greenville; puppeteer; created Bert, Ernie, Big Bird, and other Sesame Street characters, as well as Kermit the Frog, Miss Piggy, and the other Muppets

David Holmes (1770-1832), governor of Mississippi Territory (1809-17); first governor of state of Mississippi (1817-20); U.S. senator (1820-25)

Johnny Lee Hooker (1917-   ), born in Clarksdale; singer, blues guitarist; major name in rhythm-and-blues, country, rock-and-roll; wrote famous blues song "Boom Boom"

Howlin' Wolf (1910-1976), born Chester Arthur Burnett in West Point; blues singer and guitarist; versatile musician who played blues, country, and rock-and-roll music; helped develop Chicago blues

JIM HENSON

PAUL B. JOHNSON, JR.

JAMES EARL JONES

LUCIUS LAMAR

CHET LEMON

Paul B. Johnson, Sr. (1880-1943), born in Hillsboro; politician; governor (1940-43); favored free hospitalization for the poor, relief funds for the aged; signed free-textbook law; encouraged women to enter politics

Paul B. Johnson, Jr. (1916-1985), born in Hattiesburg; politician; governor (1964-68); led state to accept racial integration

Robert Johnson (1911-1938), born in Robinsville; musician; known as King of the Delta Blues; helped develop blues, country, and rock-and-roll music; known for the ferocity and force of his music; wrote the songs "Love in Vain" and "Crossroads"

William Johnson (1809-1851), born a slave; as a freedman, owned several barbershops and land in Natchez; wrote a 2,000-page diary describing antebellum life in Natchez

James Earl Jones (1931-   ), born in Arkabutla; actor; known for the versatility of his performances; won 1969 Tony Award for *The Great White Hope*; elected to Theater Hall of Fame

Belle Kearney (1863-1939), born near Vernon; writer, lecturer; wrote autobiography, *A Slaveholder's Daughter*; won seat in Mississippi state senate in 1924, becoming the first woman in the South to hold such an important position

B. B. King (1925-   ), born Riley King in Itta Bena; blues musician; called himself "Blues Boy" King; known for his playing skills on his electric guitar, "Lucille"; recorded the song "The Thrill is Gone"

Lucius Quintus Cincinnatus Lamar (1825-1893), politician, jurist; drafted Mississippi ordinance of secession but later favored reconciliation between North and South; U.S. Supreme Court justice (1888-93)

Chet Lemon (1955-   ), born in Jackson; professional baseball player; All-Star outfielder with the Chicago White Sox and the Detroit Tigers

John Avery Lomax (1872-1948), born in Goodman; folk musicologist; traveled through the country recording hundreds of songs; preserved thousands of songs in books and records

Archie Manning (1948-   ), professional football player; as quarterback at the University of Mississippi, led Ole Miss to 1970 Sugar Bowl championship; All-Pro quarterback with the New Orleans Saints, Minnesota Vikings, and Houston Oilers

James Meredith (1933-   ), born in Kosciusko; civil-rights leader; first black student to attend University of Mississippi; led 1966 civil-rights march from Memphis to Jackson

Archie Moore (1913-   ), born in Benoit; boxer; world light-heavyweight champion (1952-55)

Willie Morris (1934-   ), born in Yazoo City; author and editor; Rhodes Scholar; editor of *Harper's* Magazine; wrote autobiography *North Toward Home*

Walter Payton (1954-   ), born in Columbia; professional football player; running back, often considered the greatest all-around player in football history; starred at Jackson State University; played with the Chicago Bears (1975-87); all-time NFL rushing leader

Walker Percy (1916-1990), novelist; grew up in Greenville; wrote *The Second Coming*; won 1962 National Book Award for his novel *The Moviegoer*

William Alexander Percy (1885-1942), born in Greenville; lawyer and poet; wrote poetry collections including *In April Once, and Other Poems*; wrote *Lanterns on the Levee*, an autobiography considered an insightful portrait of Mississippi life

George Poindexter (1779-1855), statesman; governor (1820-22); distinguished jurist, congressman, and senator who almost singlehandedly shaped the first Mississippi constitution

Eliza Jane Poitevent (1849-1896), full name Eliza Jane Poitevent Holbrook Nicholson, born in Hancock County; publisher; at twenty-seven became the first woman to publish and own a large metropolitan paper in U.S. when she inherited the New Orleans *Times-Picayune*

Leontyne Price (1927-   ), born in Laurel; operatic soprano; star of New York Metropolitan Opera opening at Lincoln Center; starred as Bess in *Porgy and Bess* and Aida in *Aida*; received many Grammy awards for her operatic performances; received a Presidential Medal of Freedom (1964); received Kennedy Center Honors award (1980)

Charlie Pride (1938-   ), born in Sledge; the first successful black country-and-western singer; wrote "Kiss an Angel Good Morning"

Elvis Presley (1935-1977), born in Tupelo; singer; combined country-and-western with rhythm-and-blues sounds to create rock-and-roll; sang "Heartbreak Hotel," "Hound Dog," and "Don't Be Cruel"

Pushmataha (1764?-1824), Choctaw chief; spoke four languages; called for peace between the U.S. and Indian tribes; as a brigadier general, fought with Americans in War of 1812

John Anthony Quitman (1798-1858), soldier; commanded volunteer troops in Mexican War; led battle for Mississippi secession

Hiram Revels (1822-1901), clergyman; first black to serve in the U.S. Senate (1870-71)

Jerry Rice (1962-   ), born in Starkville; professional football player; starred at Mississippi Valley State; as wide receiver with San Francisco Forty Niners, set National Football League record for catching touchdown passes in consecutive games

WALTER PAYTON

WALKER PERCY

CHARLIE PRIDE

JOHN QUITMAN

WINTHROP SARGENT

ELIZABETH SPENCER

JOHN STENNIS

CONWAY TWITTY

Jimmie Rodgers (1897-1933), born in Meridian; country musician; known as the "Singing Brakeman" and the "Father of Country Music"; one of the first inducted into the Country Music Hall of Fame

Winthrop Sargent (1753-1820), first Mississippi territorial governor; organized court system and militia, and divided state into districts

Purvis Short (1957-   ), born in Hattiesburg; professional basketball player with the Golden State Warriors and the Houston Rockets

Elizabeth Spencer (1921-   ), born in Carrollton; author; wrote *Fire in the Morning* and other novels dealing with life in small-town Mississippi

John C. Stennis (1901-1995), born in Kemper County, politician; U.S. senator (1947-88); was a senior member of the Senate and chairman of Senate appropriations committee at his retirement

Stella Stevens (1936-   ), born Estelle Eggleston in Yazoo City; actress; starred in *L'il Abner* and *The Courtship of Eddie's Father*

William Grant Still (1895-1978), born in Woodville; composer and conductor; composed *Afro-American Symphony* (1930); first U.S. black to conduct a professional symphony orchestra (Los Angeles Symphony Orchestra, 1936)

Elizabeth Taylor (1809-1876), born in Natchez; singer; known as the "Black Swan"; appeared in a command performance before Queen Victoria of England

Ike Turner (1931-   ), born in Clarksdale, singer; teamed with Tina Turner to record "Proud Mary" and many other hit songs in the 1960s

Conway Twitty (1933-   ), born Harold Lloyd Jenkins in Friar's Point; country singer; led band, Conway Twitty and the Twitty Birds; recorded the hit song "It's Only Make Believe"

James Kimball Vardaman (1861-1930), politician; governor (1904-08); established rural and agricultural schools; U.S. senator (1912-18); campaigned as a race-baiter but took no action against blacks once in office

Robert J. Walker (1801-1869), lawyer, U.S. senator (1836-45); U.S. secretary of the treasury (1845-49); financing of Mexican War earned him nickname "Wizard of Mississippi"; first Mississippian in a presidential cabinet

Muddy Waters (1915-1983), born McKinley Morganfield in Rolling Fork; blues musician; moved to Chicago and helped establish Chicago blues; recorded "Hootchie Kootchie Man" and "Got My Mojo Workin'"; influenced Chuck Berry, the Rolling Stones, and other rock-and-roll groups

Ida B. Wells (1862-1931), born in Holly Springs; writer, civil-rights leader; fiery editor who dared to protest lynching and segregation laws; called for economic boycotts to protest inequalities; co-founder of the National Association for the Advancement of Colored People (NAACP)

Eudora Welty (1909-   ), born in Jackson; writer and critic; painted vivid pictures of southern life in her novels and short stories; traveled throughout Mississippi and wrote articles on the lives of Mississippians; received the 1973 Pulitzer Prize in fiction for *The Optimist's Daughter*

EUDORA WELTY

Frank White (1950-   ), born in Greenville; professional baseball player; All-Star second baseman with the Kansas City Royals; won seven Gold Glove awards; was voted Most Valuable Player of 1980 American League West championship playoffs

Willie White (1939-   ), born in Money; athlete, track-and-field star; won 1964 Olympic silver medal as part of 400-meter relay team

WILLIE WHITE

Jamie Whitten (1910-   ), born in Cascilla; politician; congressman (1931-33); senior member of U.S. House of Representatives; chairman of the House appropriations committee; widely respected for his knowledge of agriculture

Tennessee Williams (1911-1983), born Thomas Lanier Williams in Columbus; playwright; gained fame for harsh realism in his dramas; received the 1948 Pulitzer Prize in drama for *A Streetcar Named Desire* and the 1955 Pulitzer Prize in drama for *Cat on a Hot Tin Roof*

Oprah Winfrey (1954-   ), born in Kosciusko; television personality and actress; Academy Award nominee for her role in *The Color Purple*

JAMIE WHITTEN

Richard Wright (1908-1960), born outside Natchez, grew up in Jackson; novelist; wrote *Native Son* and *Black Boy*, an autobiography that described the poverty and racial prejudice he encountered while growing up in the South

Tammy Wynette (1942-   ), born Wynette Pugh in Tupelo; country singer; many hit songs included "Golden Rings" and "Stand by Your Man"

Emmet York (1903-1971), born in Standing Pine; educator; built Choctaw Central High School for Mississippi's Choctaw Indians; established United Southeastern Tribes, an organization to help Mississippi's Native Americans solve their problems

RICHARD WRIGHT

Stark Young (1881-1963), born in Como; author; his novels *Heaven Trees* and *So Red the Rose* are considered outstanding portrayals of life in the South

This beautifully restored Greek Revival building, now a National Historical Landmark, has been the Governor's Mansion since 1842.

GOVERNORS

David Holmes	1817-1820	Robert Lowrey	1882-1890
George Poindexter	1820-1822	John M. Stone	1890-1896
Walter Leake	1822-1825	Anselm J. McLaurin	1896-1900
Gerard C. Brandon	1825-1826	Andrew H. Longino	1900-1904
David Holmes	1826	James K. Vardaman	1904-1908
Gerard C. Brandon	1826-1832	Edmond F. Noel	1908-1912
Abram M. Scott	1832-1833	Earl L. Brewer	1912-1916
Charles Lynch	1833	Theodore G. Bilbo	1916-1920
Hiram G. Runnels	1833-1835	Lee M. Russell	1920-1924
John A. Quitman	1835-1836	Henry L. Whitfield	1924-1927
Charles Lynch	1836-1838	Dennis Murphree	1927-1928
Alexander G. McNutt	1838-1842	Theodore G. Bilbo	1928-1932
Tilghman M. Tucker	1842-1844	Martin Sennett Connor	1932-1936
Albert G. Brown	1844-1848	Hugh L. White	1936-1940
Joseph W. Matthews	1848-1850	Paul B. Johnson, Sr.	1940-1943
John A. Quitman	1850-1851	Dennis Murphree	1943-1944
John I. Guion	1851	Thomas L. Bailey	1944-1946
James Whitfield	1851-1852	Fielding L. Wright	1946-1952
Henry S. Foote	1852-1854	Hugh L. White	1952-1956
John J. Pettus	1854	James P. Coleman	1956-1960
John J. McRae	1854-1857	Ross R. Barnett	1960-1964
William McWillie	1857-1859	Paul B. Johnson, Jr.	1964-1968
John J. Pettus	1859-1863	John Bell Williams	1968-1972
Charles Clark	1863-1865	William Waller	1972-1976
William J. Sharkey	1865	Cliff Finch	1976-1980
Benjamin G. Humphreys	1865-1868	William F. Winter	1980-1984
Adelbert Ames	1868-1870	William A. Allain	1984-1988
James L. Alcorn	1870-1871	Ray Mabus, Jr.	1988-1992
Ridgley C. Powers	1871-1874	Kirk Fordice	1992-
Adelbert Ames	1874-1876		
John M. Stone	1876-1882		

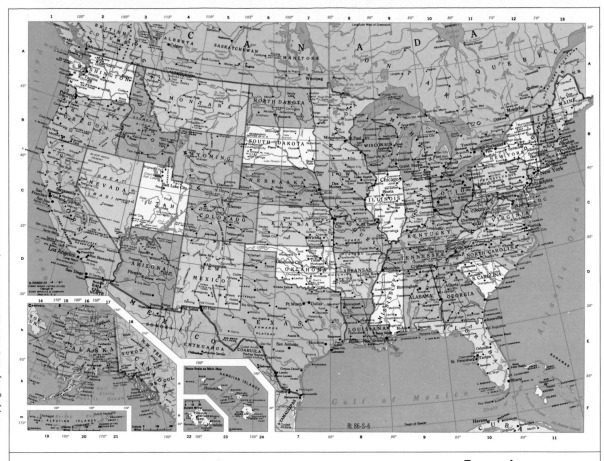

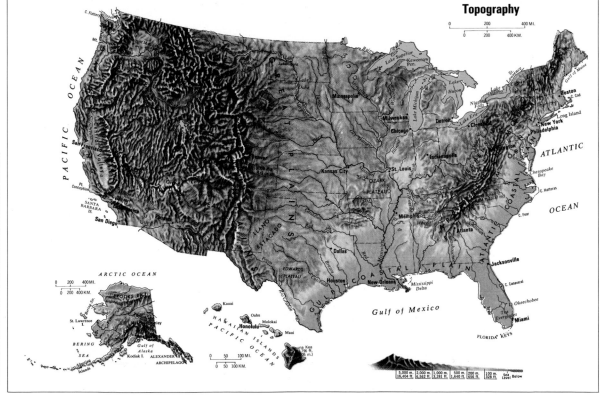

Topography

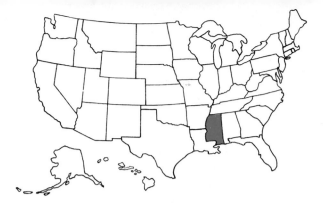

MAP KEY

Abbeville	A4
Aberdeen	B5
Ackerman	B4
Adams	C3
Alcorn College	D2
Alligator	A3
Amory	B5
Anguilla	C3
Arcola	B3
Arkabutla Lake (lake)	A3
Artesia	B5
Ashland	A4
Avalon	B2
Baldwyn	A5
Bassfield	D4
Batesville	A4
Bay Springs	D4
Bay St. Louis	D4;g7
Bayou Pierre (bayou)	D3
Bear Creek (creek)	A5
Bear Town	D3
Beaumont	D5
Beauregard	D3
Bellefontaine	B4
Belmont	A5
Belzoni	B3
Benoit	B2
Bentonia	C3
Beulah	B3
Beulah Lake (lake)	B2
Big Black River (river)	B4;C2,3,4
Big Creek	B4
Big Creek (creek)	D5
Big Sunflower River (river)	B,C3
Biloxi	E5;f8
Biloxi Bay (bay)	f8
Biloxi River (river)	E4
Black Creek (creek)	D,E4,5
Black Hawk	B3
Blue Mountain	A4
Blue Springs	A5
Bogue Chitto River (river)	D3
Bogue Phalia River (river)	B3
Bolton	C3
Booneville	A5
Bowie Creek (creek)	D4
Boyle	B3
Brandon	C4
Braxton	C4
Brookhaven	D3
Brooksville	B5
Bruce	B4
Buckatunna	D5
Bude	D3
Burns	C4
Burnsville	A5
Buttahatchee River (river)	B5
Byhalia	A4
Caledonia	B5
Calhoun City	B4
Canton	C3
Carrollton	B4
Carthage	C4
Cary	C3
Cat Island (island)	E4;g7
Cedarbluff	B5
Centreville	D2
Charleston	A3
Chickasawhay River (river)	C,D,E5
Choctaw Indian Reservation	C4
Chunky	C5
Clarksdale	A3
Cleveland	B3
Clinton	C3
Coffeeville	B4
Coldwater	A4
Coldwater River (river)	A3
Collins	D4
Columbia	D4
Columbus	B5
Columbus Air Force Base	B5
Como	A4
Conehatta	C4
Corinth	A5
Courtland	A4
Crawford	B5
Crenshaw	A3
Crosby	D2
Crowder	A3
Cruger	B3
Crystal Springs	D3
Decatur	C4
Deer Creek (creek)	B,C3
Deer Island (island)	f8
De Kalb	C5
Delta (geological area)	A,B,C3
Derby	E4
Derma	B4
D'Iberville	E5;f8
D'Lo	D4
Doddsville	B3
Dog Keys Pass (channel)	g8
Drew	B3
Duck Hill	B4
Dumas	A5
Duncan	A3
Durant	B4
Eagle Lake (lake)	C2,3
Ecru	A4
Eden	C3
Edinburg	C4
Edwards	C3
Elizabeth	B3
Ellisville	D4
Enid Lake (lake)	A4
Enterprise	C5
Escatawpa	E5;f8
Escatawpa River (river)	E5
Ethel	B4
Eupora	B4
Evergreen	A5
Falcon	A3
Falkner	A5
Fayette	D2
Flora	C3
Florence	C3
Flowood	C3
Forest	C4
French Camp	B4
Friars Point	A3
Fulton	A5
Gattman	B5
Gautier	f8
Georgetown	D3
Glendale	D4
Glendora	B3
Gloster	D2
Golden	A5
Good Hope	C4
Goodman	C4
Greenville	B2
Greenwood	B3
Grenada	B4
Grenada Lake (lake)	B4
Gulf Islands National Seashore	E5;g8,9
Gulf of Mexico	E4,5;g7,8,9
Gulfport	E4;f7
Gunnison	B3
Guntown	A5
Hatley	B5
Hattiesburg	D4
Hazelhurst	D3
Heidelberg	D5
Henderson Point (point)	g7
Henderson's Point	g7
Hernando	A4
Hickory	C4
Hickory Flat	A4
Hillsboro	C4
Hiwannee	D5
Hollandale	B3
Holly Bluff	C3
Holly Springs	A4
Homochitto River (river)	D2,3
Horn Island (island)	E5;g8
Horn Island Pass (channel)	g8,9
Horn Lake	A3
Horn Lake (lake)	A3
Hot Coffee	D4
Houlka	A4
Houston	B4
Indianola	B3
Inverness	B3
Isola	B3
Itta Bena	B3
Iuka	A5
Jackson	C3
Jonestown	A3
Jonestown	C3
Keesler Air Force Base	E5;f8
Kewanee	C5
Kilmichael	B4
Kings	C3
Kosciusko	B4
Kossuth	A5
Lake	C4
Lake Bolivar (lake)	B2
Lake Lee (lake)	B2
Lake Mary (lake)	D2
Lake Washington (lake)	B2
Lambert	A3
Laurel	D4
Le Tourneau	C3
Leaf River (river)	C,D4,5
Leakesville	D5
Learned	C3
Leland	B3
Lena	C4
Lexington	B3
Liberty	D3
Long Beach	E4;f7
Louin	C4
Louise	C3
Louisville	B4
Lucedale	E5
Lucien	D3
Lula	A3
Lumberton	D,E4
Lyon	A3
Maben	B4
Macon	B5
Madison	C3
Magee	D4
Magnolia	D3
Mantachie	A5
Mantee	B4
Marietta	A5
Marion	C5
Marks	A3
Mathiston	B4
Mayersville	C2
McCarley	B4
McComb	D3
McCool	B4
McLain	D5
Meadville	D3
Mendenhall	D4
Meridian	C5
Meridian Naval Air Station	C5
Merigold	B3
Metcalfe	B2,3
Midnight	B3
Mineral Wells	A4
Mississippi River (river)	A2,3,4;B2;C2,3;D2
Mississippi Sound (sound)	E5;g7,8,9
Mize	D4
Monticello	D3
Montrose	C4
Moon Lake (lake)	A3
Moorhead	B3
Morgan City	B3
Morgantown	D2
Morgantown	D4
Morton	C4
Moss Point	E5;f8
Mound Bayou	B3
Mount Olive	D4
Mount Pleasant	A4
Myrtle	A4
Natchez	D2
Nettleton	A5
New Albany	A4
New Augusta	D4
Newton	C4
Nitta Yuma	B3
North Carrollton	B4
North Gulfport	E4;f7
Noxapater	C4
Noxubee River (river)	B,C4,5
Oakland	A4
Ocean Springs	E5;f8
Ofahoma	C4
Oil City	C3
Okatibbee Creek (creek)	C5
Okatoma Creek (creek)	D4
Okolona	A,B5
Olive Branch	A4
Orange Grove	E5;f8,9
Osyka	D3
Oxford	A4
Pace	B3
Pachuta	C5
Paden	A5
Palmers Crossing	D4
Pascagoula	E5;f8
Pascagoula Bay (bay)	f8
Pascagoula River (river)	E5
Pass Christian	E4;g7
Pearl	C3
Pearl River (river)	C3,4;D3,4;E4
Pelahatchie	C4
Petal	D4
Petit Bois Island (island)	E5;g9
Philadelphia	C4
Picayune	E4
Pickens	C4
Piney Woods	C4
Pittsboro	B4
Plantersville	A5
Pleasant Grove	A3
Polkville	C4
Pontotoc	A4
Pope	A4
Poplarville	E4
Port Gibson	D3
Potts Camp	A4
Prairie Point	B5
Prentiss	D4
Puckett	C4
Purvis	D4
Quitman	C5
Raleigh	C4
Raymond	C3
Red Creek (creek)	E4,5
Redwood	C3
Richton	D5
Ridgeland	C3
Rienzi	A5
Ripley	A5
Rolling Fork	C3
Rosedale	B2
Ross Barnett Reservoir (reservoir)	C3,4
Rough Edge	A5
Round Island (island)	g8
Roxie	D2
Ruleville	B3
St. Louis Bay (bay)	f,g7
Sallis	B4
Saltillo	A5
Sandersville	D4
Sandhill	C4
Sandy Hook	D4
Sardis	A4
Sardis Lake (lake)	A4
Satartia	C3
Schlater	B3
Scooba	C5
Sebastopol	C4
Seminary	D4
Senatobia	A4
Shannon	A5
Shaw	B3
Shelby	B3
Sherman	A5
Ship Island (island)	E5;g8
Ship Island Pass (channel)	g7,8
Shubuta	D5
Shuford	A4
Shuqualak	C5
Sidon	B3
Silver City	B3
Silver Creek	D3
Skuna River (river)	A,B4
Slate Spring	B4
Sledge	A3
Smithville	A5
Sontag	D3
Soso	D4
Southaven	A3
Stanton	D2
Starkville	B5
State College	B5
State Line	D5
Stonewall	C5
Strayhorn	A3
Strong River (river)	C,D4
Sturgis	B4
Sucarnoochee River (river)	C5
Summit	D3
Sumner	B3
Sumrall	D4
Sunflower	B3
Sylvarena	C4
Tallahala Creek (creek)	D4
Tallahatchie River (river)	A3,4;B,C3
Taylor	A4
Taylorsville	D4
Tchula	B3
Terry	C3
Thaxton	A4
Theadville	D5
Thompson Creek (creek)	D5
Three Rivers	E5
Tillatoba	B4
Tippah Creek (creek)	A4
Tishomingo	A5
Toccopola	A4
Tombigbee River (river)	A,B5
Tremont	A5
Tunica	A3
Tupelo	A5
Tuscola	C4
Tutwiler	A3
Tylertown	D3
Union Church	D3
Utica	C3
Vaiden	B4
Vancleave	E5
Vardaman	B4
Vaughan	C3
Verona	A5
Vicksburg	C3
Vicksburg National Military Park	C3
Walnut	A5
Walnut Grove	C4
Walthall	B4
Washington	D2
Water Valley	A4
Waveland	E4;g7
Waynesboro	D5
Wayside	B2
Webb	B3
Weir	B4
Wenasoga	A5
Wesson	D3
West	B4
West Point	B5
Winona	B4
Winstonville	B2
Wolf River (river)	E4;f7
Woodall Mountain (mountain)	A5
Woodland	B4
Woodville	D2
Wool Market	E4;f7
Yalobusha River (river)	B3,4
Yazoo City	C3
Yazoo River (river)	B,C3
Yockanookany River (river)	B,C4
Yocona River (river)	A4
Zama	C4

TENNESSEE

ARKANSAS

LOUISIANA

ALABAMA

Memphis

W. Memphis

Forrest City

Jacksonville

Stuttgart

Pine Bluff

Helena

Greenville

Greenwood

Yazoo City

Canton

Jackson

Vicksburg

Tallulah

Monroe

Natchez

Brookhaven

Hattiesburg

Laurel

Meridian

Columbus

Starkville

State College

Tupelo

Corinth

Florence

Sheffield

Tuscumbia

Russellville

Bastrop

Gulfport

Biloxi

Pascagoula

Mobile

PICKWICK LANDING DAM

SHILOH NAT. MIL. PARK & CEMETERY

HIGHEST POINT IN MISSISSIPPI

VICKSBURG NAT. MIL. PARK

GULF ISLANDS NATIONAL SEASHORE

Mississippi Sound

Gulf of Mexico

Lambert Conformal Conic Projection

Statute Miles

Longitude West of Greenwich

Copyright by RAND McNALLY & COMPANY.
Made in U.S.A.

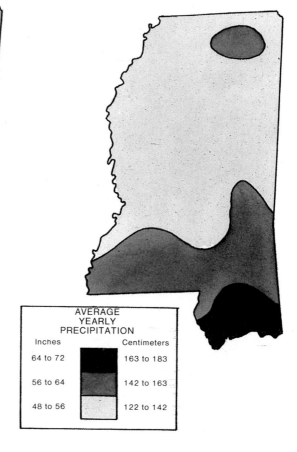

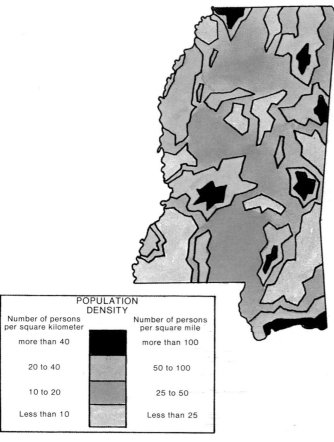

POPULATION DENSITY

Number of persons per square kilometer		Number of persons per square mile
more than 40		more than 100
20 to 40		50 to 100
10 to 20		25 to 50
Less than 10		Less than 25

AVERAGE YEARLY PRECIPITATION

Inches		Centimeters
64 to 72		163 to 183
56 to 64		142 to 163
48 to 56		122 to 142

 POULTRY

HOGS

BEEF

DAIRY PRODUCTS

CORN

OATS

RICE

COTTON

SOYBEANS

SWEET POTATOES
VEGETABLES

PECANS

HONEY

FRUIT

FISH

SHRIMP

OYSTERS

OIL

NATURAL GAS

 FOREST PRODUCTS

MAJOR HIGHWAYS

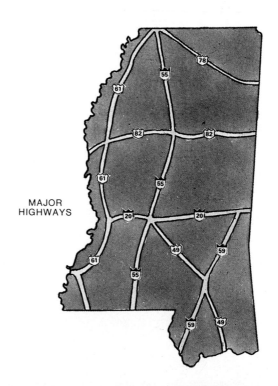

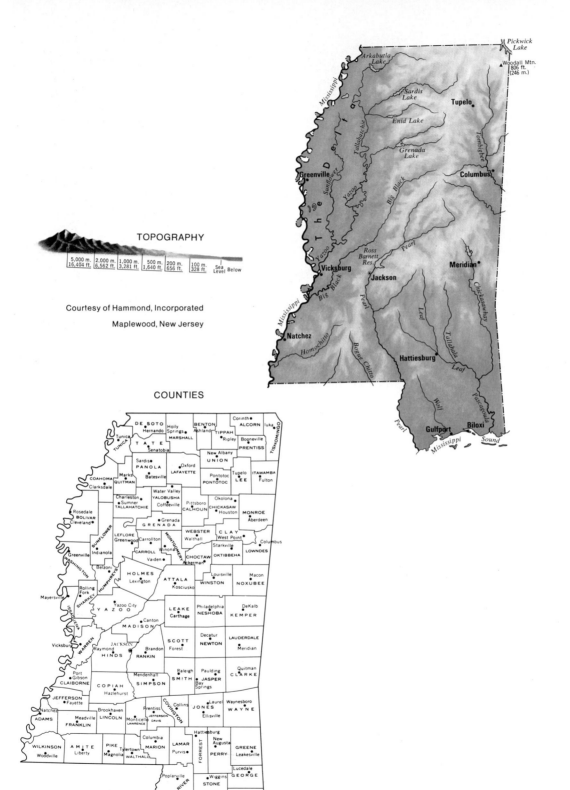

TOPOGRAPHY

5,000 m. | 2,000 m. | 1,000 m. | 500 m. | 200 m. | 100 m. | Sea
16,404 ft. | 6,562 ft. | 3,281 ft. | 1,640 ft. | 656 ft. | 328 ft. | Level | Below

Courtesy of Hammond, Incorporated

Maplewood, New Jersey

COUNTIES

Melrose, set in lovely old gardens, is one of the most beautiful antebellum homes in Natchez.

INDEX

Page numbers that appear in boldface type indicate illustrations.

139

King's Tavern, in Natchez, began serving the public in 1789.

Picture Identifications

Front cover: Longwood House, Natchez
Back cover: A shrimp boat at sunset
Pages 2-3: The Biloxi Lighthouse
Page 6: Mississippi magnolia blossoms
Pages 8-9: A Mississippi River oxbow
Pages 18-19: A montage of Mississippians
Pages 26-27: The Old Spanish Fort in Pascagoula
Page 35: *Low Water on the Mississippi*, a Currier and Ives lithograph
Pages 44-45: The Union attack at Vicksburg
Page 56: Rice harvesting
Page 70: The State Capitol, Jackson
Pages 80-81: Mynelle Gardens, Jackson
Pages 94-95: The *Mississippi Queen*
Page 108: Montage showing the state flag, the state bird (mockingbird), the state tree (magnolia), and the state flower (magnolia blossom)

About the Author

Robert Carson was born in Michigan. He received a Bachelor of Arts degree in English from the University of Michigan at Ann Arbor. As a child, he toured the nation as an actor with a traveling theater group. Mississippi became one of his favorite states. Mr. Carson has written ten novels, plays for children's theater, and short stories that have appeared in *The Atlantic* and *Cosmopolitan*. He now lives in Mexico.